Classic Carved Furniture

MAKING A PIECRUST TEA TABLE

Tom Heller & Ron Clarkson

A step-by-step guide to creating an American Classic

77 Lower Valley Road, Atglen, PA 19310

Text written with & photography by Douglas Congdon-Martin

Copyright © 1994 by
Tom Heller and Ron Clarkson
Library of Congress Catalog Number: 94-65627

Printed in The United States of America
ISBN: 0-88740-616-5

We are interested in hearing from authors
with book ideas on related topics.

Published by Schiffer Publishing Ltd.
77 Lower Valley Road
Atglen, PA 19310
Please write for a free catalog.
This book may be purchased from the publisher.
Please include $2.95 postage.
Try your bookstore first.

Contents

Introduction

Grace and elegance are the hallmarks of the pie crust tea table. Beautiful as well as functional, it was the centerpiece of eighteenth century sociability.

Its design reflects its main purpose: serving tea. As with all things utilitarian, it was a product of its time. In eighteenth century America, tea was an integral part of the social and political fabric of our country. Afternoon tea was a time for gathering, for sharing news, and for conducting the affairs of the community in an informal, but influential way. At these teas the hostess would bring the table out to serve her guests. She would sit at the table, pour tea and rotate the table to serve her guests. Each would receive a cup in this manner until all had been served. No one had to stand to pour or reach to serve.

It was important to have the finest elements for serving tea. From the imported cups and saucers, to the silver teas service, to the beautifully carved table, the quality of the service reflected on the status of the host. During tea time the table would stand at the center of activity, and could be easily seen and admired by all in attendance. Afterwards, the top of the table could be tilted into an upright position and easily moved to a lesser used part of the room for storage. There it would stand elegant and ready for the next occasion.

There was, in fact, much to admire in a table such as this one. The top was beautifully sculpted with curves and moldings. It rested on an open style birdcage, a thing of beauty and some engineering. This rotated on a finely contoured and turned pillar adorned at the vase with acanthus leaves balancing on a delicate ring of pearls, which ended in a ribbon and flower design. The whole table is supported by three finely carved cabriole legs, which, again, are adorned with life-like acanthus leaves, ending in a strongly taloned ball and claw foot. The use of Hogarth's "line of beauty," the cyma curve, is quite evident throughout.

Today the table can be used as an ornamental piece or as an occasional table. Depending on your decor, this table will look just as lovely in the serving position with a lamp or vase resting gracefully upon its scalloped top, or standing in a corner of the room, showing off the beauty of the top and the forceful grace of the finely carved legs.

On the cover of this book we have used a very figured piece of crotch mahogany for the top of the table. Its purpose is to accentuate the importance of the overall piece, but it is a rare wood and not necessary for a beautiful table. The top we used to demonstrate the process building the table, was of straight grained mahogany. Remember, the more figured the wood, the higher level of difficulty in carving.

Whatever elements you choose to use, your project will turn out well if you follow the basic guidelines we've shown here. The purpose of this book is to bring to you a fine example of pure American Rococo carving. With patience and practice, we believe the pie crust tea table you build will bring many compliments and hours of joy to you.

Acknowledgements

We wish to thank Jody Garrett and Woodcraft Supply Corporation of Parksburg, West Virginia, the Dewalt Tool Company, James A. Guthrie and Wagner Spray Tech, for their assistance in making this book possible.

Most importantly, we thank Peter Schiffer, Douglas Congdon-Martin, and all the fine people at Schiffer Publishing Company, Ltd., for helping us to realize a dream.

The Piecrust Tea Table

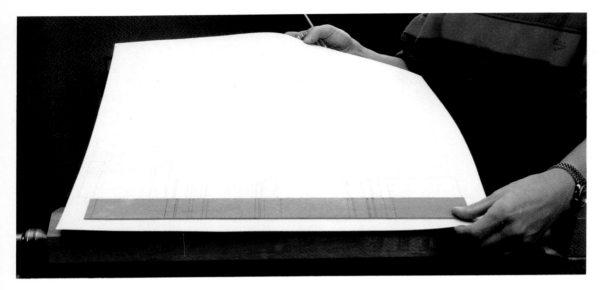

Make a full-size drawing of the post, and on a strip of wood layout the divisions of the turning on the stock.

The billet is 25 inches long and four inches square. If you can't find a piece four inches thick you can glue up two pieces.

After finding the center of the end, I scribe a four-inch circle. This gives me the guidelines I need for knocking off the corners at a 45 degree angle, which makes the turning easier.

Turn the billet round all the way down.

When you get to round you can go back and smooth the cut.

This may take several passes.

Ready for shaping.

Stop and check your progress. This end needs a little more work.

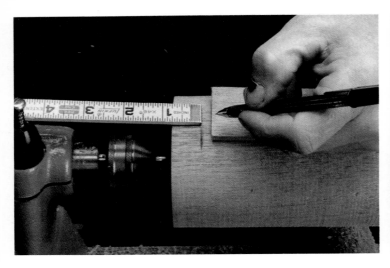

From the end measure 3/4" and make a mark. This mark will be the bottom of the pedestal.

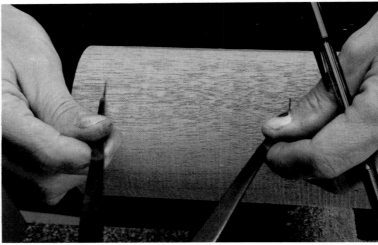

The dividers can also be used to check the marks you make with the pattern stick method.

Lay the pattern stick on the mark and transfer the lines of the turning segments to the billet.

We begin by turning a trunnion at the base of the pedestal. This will hold it in a jig for dovetailing. It is 1 1/4" inches in diameter, and, as we already marked, 3/4" long. Scribe the line with the point of the parting tool.

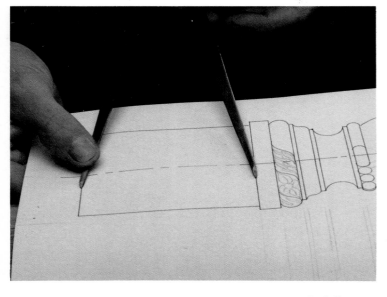

You can also use dividers to transfer the pattern to the billet.

Take the trunnion down with the cutting edge of the parting tool.

A caliper will help you get it to size

Next we set the depths of the various segments. I begin with the two fillets on either side of the cove. They are set to a depth of 2 13/16". I start here, because starting elsewhere would cause me to lose my lines. Cut right across the cove.

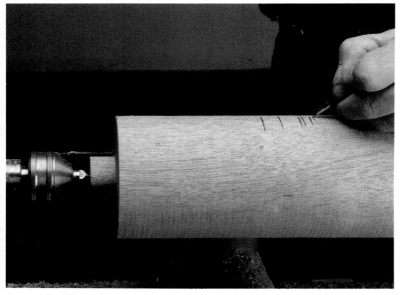

The trunnion formed.

Measure the diameter. I prefer to stop the lathe to do this for safety's sake.

Score the remaining segment lines with the parting tool.

Continue to cut and measure...

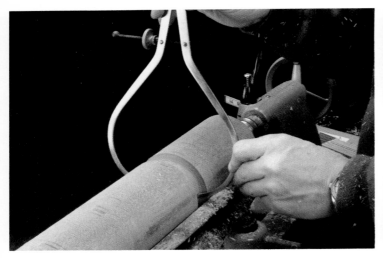

until you get to the correct depth.

Moving up set the bead above the cove at 3".

Moving toward the base, set the adjacent fillet at 3 5/16".

Progress. Note that while we are setting depths, everything stays square.

Measure with the caliper.

Now we move above the vase segment and start setting the depths of the column. We will set the bead above the vase at 2 5/8".

8

Move up to the last bead of the column and define it at 2 1/2" diameter. Because the last cut was to 2 5/8", you can almost eyeball this diameter.

Progress.

Progress.

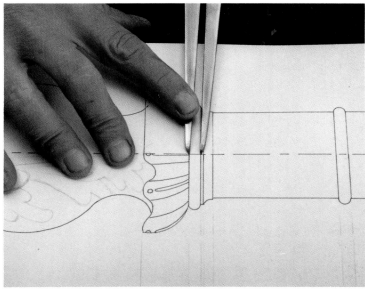

We need to reestablish our lines. You can't use the pattern stick here, so set your dividers to the drawing. Set the caliper to the thickness of the bead above the vase.

With a large gouge rough down the column section, between the two partings you just made.

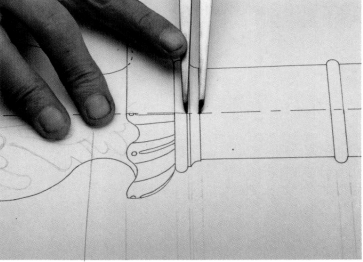

This same thickness will also define the cove above the bead.

9

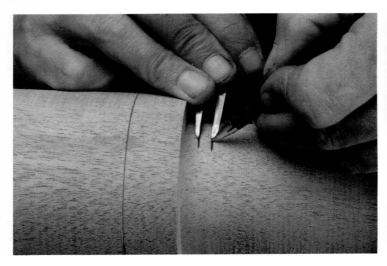

Mark them on the column.

Set the depths with the parting tool. Start with the fillet above the bottom bead. This will be 2 1/2".

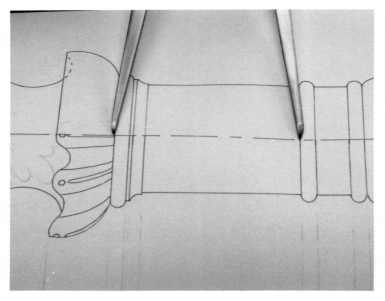

Measure all the other distances of the column from the bottom of the bead above the vase. This will help insure accuracy.

Establish the base of the flat area above the cove at 2 1/4".

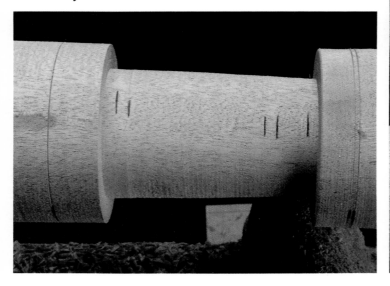

The column marked.

Below the next bead the column will be 2 3/16" in diameter.

Mark the line with the parting tool and take it down to the correct depth.

Continuing to work our way up, we relieve the wood between the two beads.

With a medium gouge, take down the flat area between the areas you have just established. With this cut the tool rest is pretty far away from the cut, increasing the chances that the tool will catch. Be very careful!

This will take you to this point.

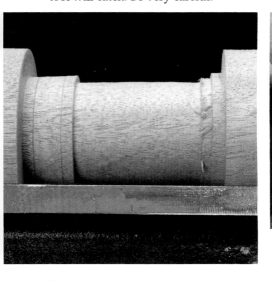

Progress.

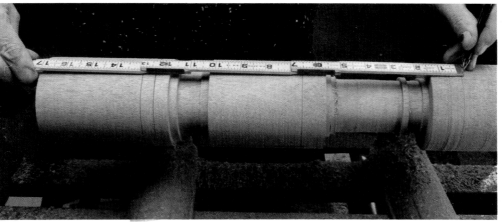

Before going further, I always check my overall measurement. I want the column to be 17 1/8", but it is only 17 1/16". I probably cut a little too far when creating the trunnion. Add any necessary length to the top.

I'm not going to turn the post that goes into the birdcage yet, but I am going to turn it enough to establish its position. If I turned now it would be a weak point in the work, and would effect other turnings.

The fillet is 3 5/16" in diameter.

Turn the end of the billet to 3 1/2".

Turn the area of the cove down to the same diameter.

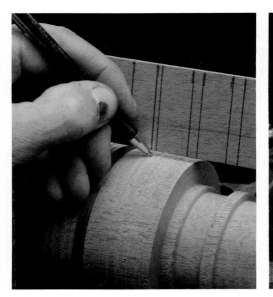

Use the pattern stick to establish the fillet line at the cap of the column.

The depths of the turnings are established.

Now we establish the profiles of the segments. This is done largely by eye, and what I do is look over the top of the turning as I go.

The result.

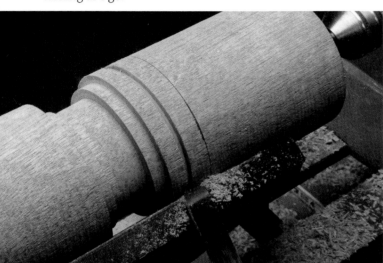

Begin with the parting tool at the large bead at the bottom of the post. I hold the tool so the bottom edge goes into the turning perpendicular. The top edge then is about 45 degrees. This does two things. It establishes the flat edge of the collar beneath the bead, and begins to establish the shape of the bead.

Switch to a small gouge to turn the ogee.

With the parting tool round the bead.

This establishes the fillet above the bead and the lower, cove part of the ogee curve.

The parting tool can be used to complete the upper, convex part of the ogee curve.

The result.

The result. In fine furniture turning, crispness counts.

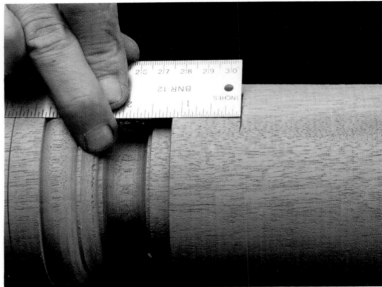

The bulbous part of the vase is basically a 4" ball. We need to find the center of the ball. It is 1 1/8" above the lower edge we established for the vase.

Next is the large cove. We need to keep in mind the depth at its center. This will be 2 1/4". With a medium gouge work carefully from side to side across the cove to establish the shape and the depth you want. At the same time you will be creating fillets above and below the cove. This is a tight cut and without proper caution, it is easy to catch the corner of the tool in the wood.

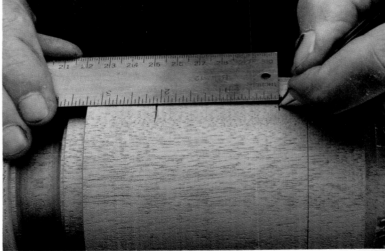

Measure from the same spot up 3 1/4" to set the center of the cove of the vase.

Round the bottom of the vase. I use a beveled parting tool for this cut.

Defined.

Progress.

Round the bead under the vase.

Use a smaller parting tool to define the top of the bead.

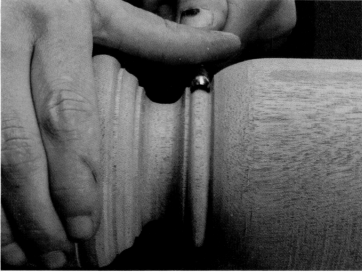

This bead is to be a carved element. so before going too far, I need to check to see if the bead matches my carving tool.

Adjust the bead...

With a medium gouge start at the line for the top of the vase and work to the deepest point. This will be at a final diameter of 2 1/8".

until it matches.

Progress.

Before going further, do a final cut with a carving tool, turning the post by hand.

Now we need to round the bulbous part of the base to blend with the narrow part.

Continue to round out from the center, above and below.

The result.

The result.

Round over the top of the vase.

Undercut the lip of the vase.

The result. This top is a carved segment.

Next we shape the bead above the vase. With a parting tool define the separation between the vase and the bead.

This is the result.

Then round over the bead, using the flat edge of the point.

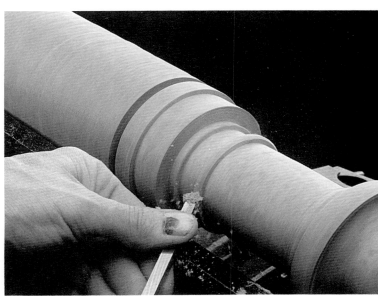

Round over the next bead with a parting tool.

A small gouge then creates the cove above the bead, leaving a fillet between.

A reversed ogee tops the post. Begin by establishing the fillet under the collar.

Curve down to the bead below the ogee.

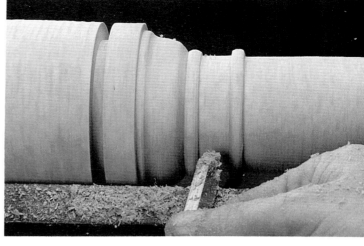

Round the bead.

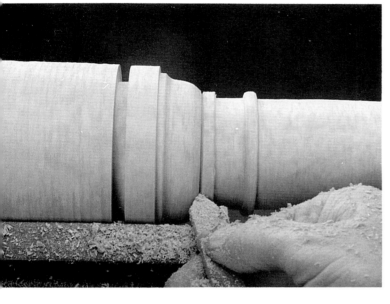

Define the separation between the ogee and the bead with a parting tool...

The result.

and round the curve into it.

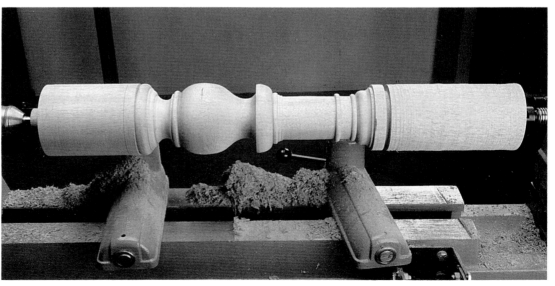

The basic turning is done.

Next we take the lower section, where the legs will be joined, to its final diameter, 3 5/8". Set the diameter with a parting tool.

Holding a straight edge along the turning will help me see where the final corrections need to be made.

It is important that the diameter be consistent through this whole section so you have a nice smooth area for the legs to fit against. To do this I establish three rings to the proper depth using a parting tool...

I do the final cut with a flat chisel.

then take the whole area to the same diameter using a gouge.

This Forstner bit will create the hole for the birdcage, so we use it as a guide to set the caliper to establish the diameter of the post that goes through the birdcage.

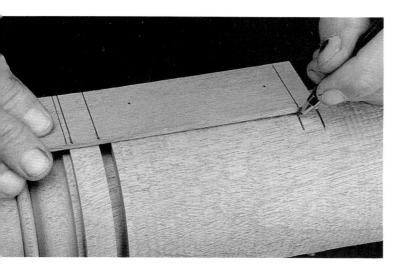

Use the pattern stick to reestablish and mark the length of the post.

and keep checking.

A parting tool establishes the depth.

Go to the end of the turning and take it to the same diameter.

It is important that this be an accurate fit or the birdcage will have unwanted movement. Take small cuts...

With these two ends set...

we remove most of the waste between with the gouge.

The result.

This needs to be straight, so check it with the calipers.

Score a line 1/2" from the end. The last 1/2" of the post goes down to 1" in diameter, creating a tenon that fits into the top of the bird cage.

The final cut is with the straight chisel.

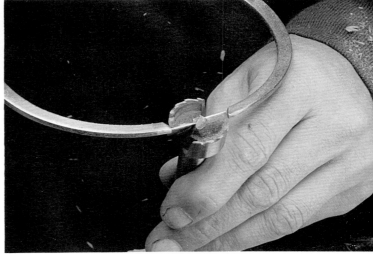

The hole in the top of the birdcage will be set with a bit. Use this bit to set the calipers.

I cut the tenon with a parting tool. As I look over the profile of the piece while its turning I want to create a cut 1/4" deep. Thinking about this helps me judge the result.

Define the upper edge with the parting tool.

The result.

The first fillet is 3 1/4" in diameter. Cut it with the parting tool

The post turning is complete. All that is left is to turn the keeper ring from the block at the top.

The other fillet is 2 11/16".

The result.

Finished.

Cut an ogee curve between the fillets, starting with the cove, using a gouge...

Sanding begins with 80 grit paper and light pressure. Always remember to have your hands under the turning.

and rounding the top with a parting tool.

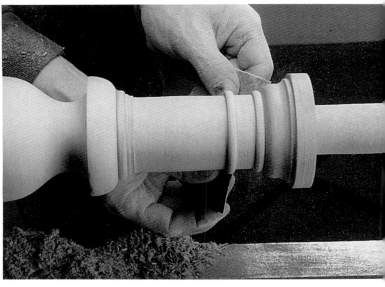

Always keep the paper moving.

Switch to 150 grit paper and go over the piece again.

Finally, go over it with Scotchbrite™ pad (no soap!).

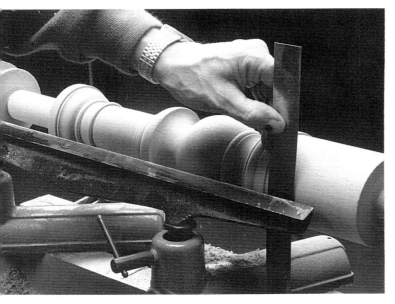

Align the tool rest with the center of the post.

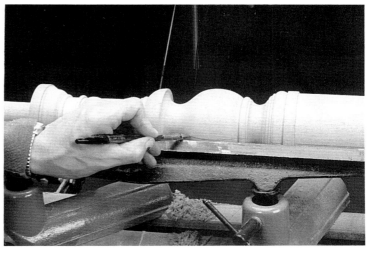

Mark a line down the center.

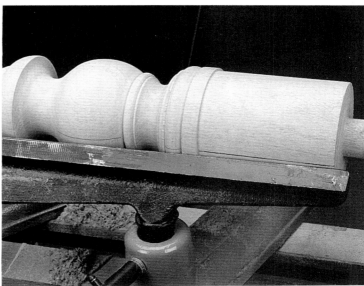

This line is the base for positioning the legs and the carvings. The other two legs and carving patterns are 120 degrees each side of this line.

With an indexing head like this lathe has, it is easy to determine the positions. There are 60 holes in the head, so 20 holes is a third of the way around the circle or 120 degrees. Mark one 120 degree line and turn the post another 20 holes and mark again.

The top of the vase is gadrooned. It is marked in twenty segments, using the indexing head. This number can vary, but it needs to be an even number. With the indexed head make one mark every three holes.

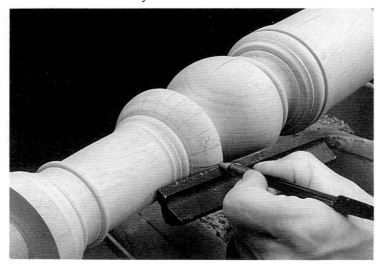

Work your way around the top of the vase.

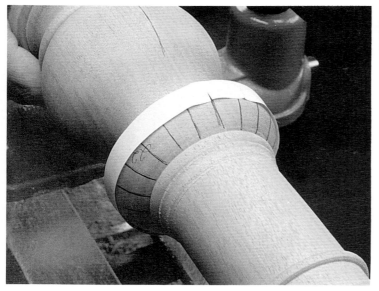

If you do not have an indexing head put a piece of tape around the circumference and cut it to fit exactly.

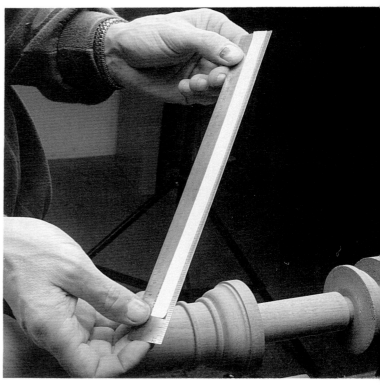

Remove the tape, measure it, and divide it into 20 equal pieces. Lay the tape back on the post and use it as your guide.

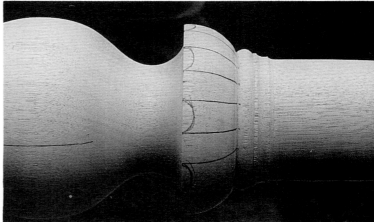

Every other segment will be a cove.

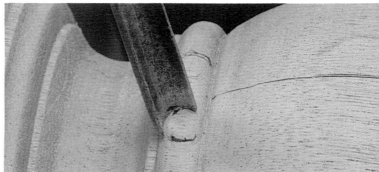

You established the bead below the vase using a chisel. Use the same chisel to create the "pearls" along the beading. Walk it around...

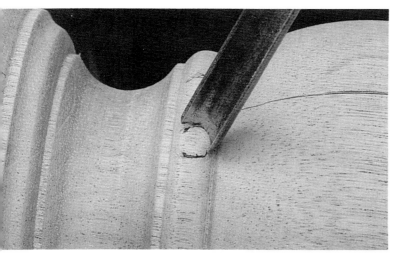

to establish...

a pearl.

Lay down three pearls end to end.

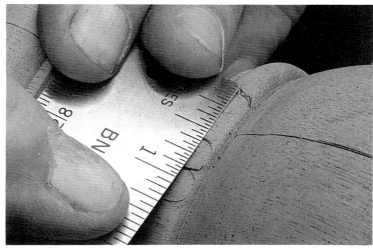

Measure the set of three. Here it is 7/8".

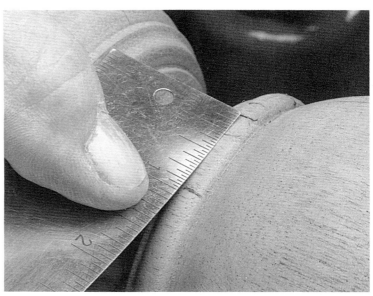

Mark segments of 7/8" around the bead. This is kind of a test fit, and it shows that I will be pretty close, needing only to stretch a little between pearls for a perfect fit. If you are way off, you will need to use a different sized gouge.

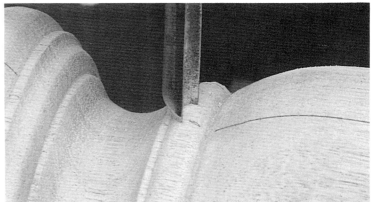

The pattern for the bead is three "pearls" and one lozenge the length of three pearls. I walk this off with the gouge, pressing hard on the groups of three that will be permanently, and lightly on the groups of three that will become a smooth lozenge.

Mark the beads and lozenges.

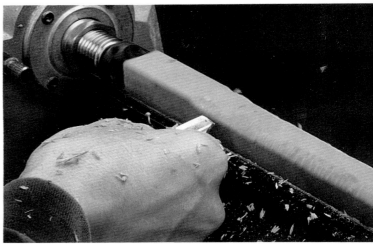

Begin by taking the blank to round.

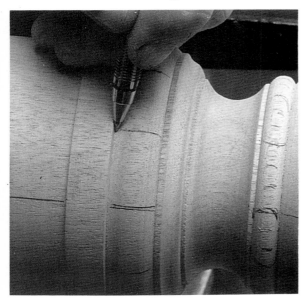

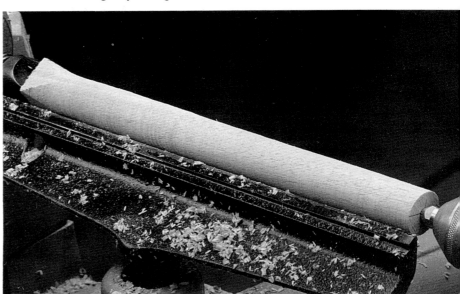

Next we need to lay out the flower and the rope. There are six flowers and six ropes. The indexing head should make this easy. With 60 stops in the head, we need to mark every 5 stops. Start at one of the main lines.

Progress.

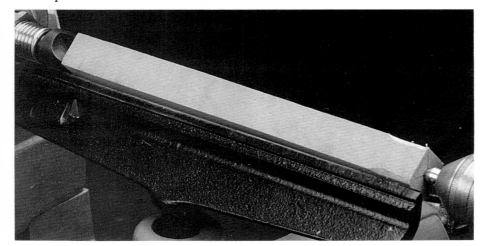

The spindles for the bird cage are turned from 1" x 1" stock. We get two spindles from each 10 1/2" stick. If you try to do all four from one stick you get too much movement.

Transfer the segments of the spindle to the pattern board, and mark them on the blank. I do one spindle at a time.

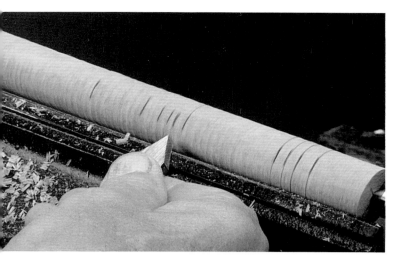

Use the parting tool to score the lines.

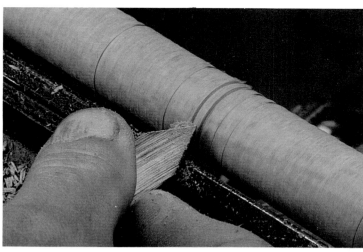

At the bottom of the spindle define the ring with the parting tool...

Form the ring at the top of the spindle.

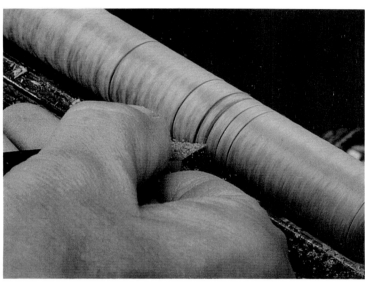

and rounding it over.

Round the top of the vase down to it.

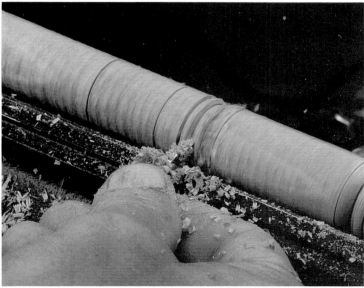

Take the fillet it above this ring to 7/8".

Progress.

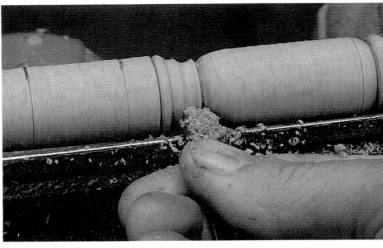

Create a cove in the segment beneath the vase, using a gouge.

Set the depth at the bottom of the vase...

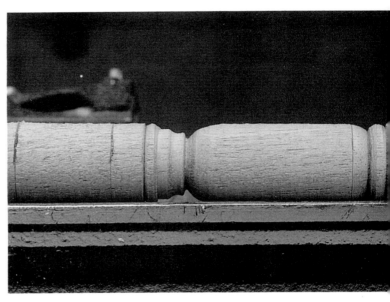

Progress.

and round the bottom of the vase down to it.

Set the depth of the cove part of the vase at 9/16".

The result.

Cut the tenons to 5/8", top...

Round of the bulb of the base, blending it into the cove.

and bottom.

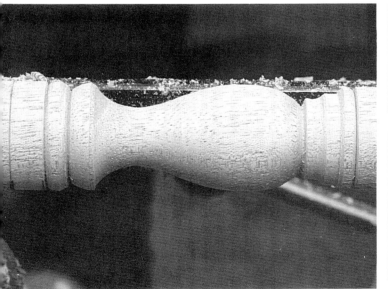

Result.

The turning done and ready for sanding. Repeat the process for the other three spindles.

This jig for dovetailing the pedestal is built from scrap materials. Plans are found in the back of the book.

The pedestal goes in the box with the bottom trunnion in the hole at the bottom of the box.

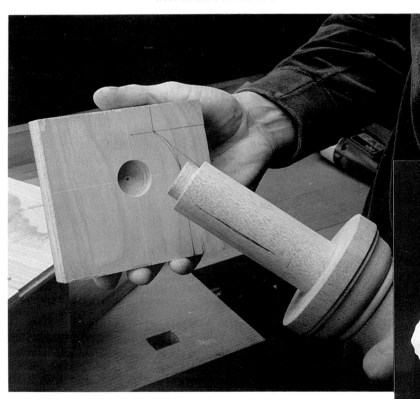

This piece fits on the top trunnion.

Place two screws to hold the top plate in place.

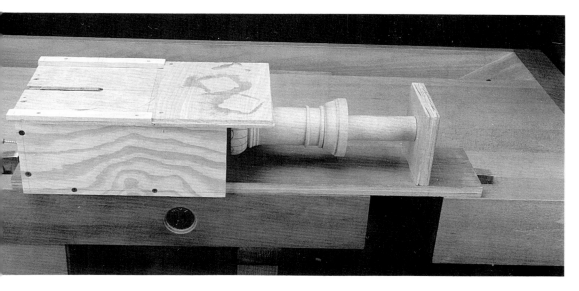

Secure the jig to the bench.

The dovetails are cut with a router, using a 7/8" dovetailing bit.

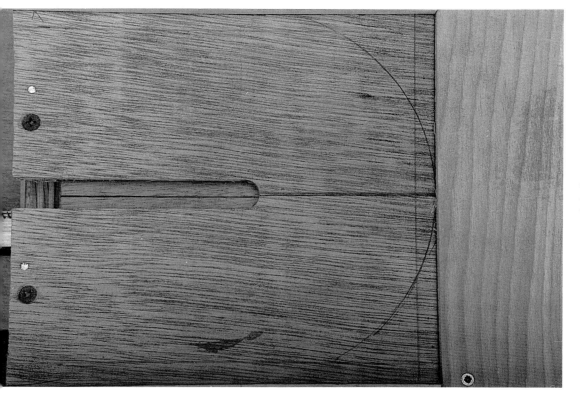

The line on the jig aligns with the line we drew on the base of the table pedestal.

The screw at the bottom is a set screw. Once your alignment is correct it is very important to hold the pedestal in place with this screw before routing.

Adjust the bit in the router so it clears the jig and matches the dovetail position in the jig.

Run the router up the slot. Go slow to get a nice even cut.

The result.

With the pedestal secured in an Easly vise we begin carving the decorative work. Start at the gadrooning. We'll carve the concave segments first. Find a gouge that most nearly matches the width of the segment. You'll need to change direction to go with the grain.

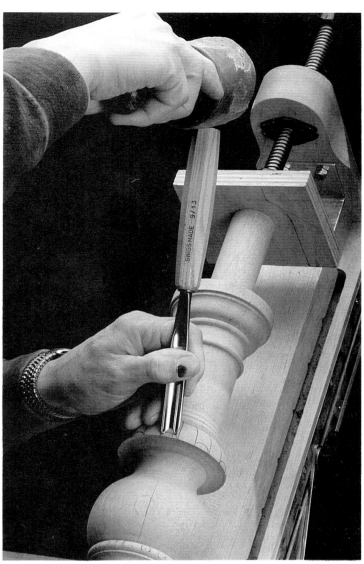

Out of the jig. Repeat at the other two dovetails.

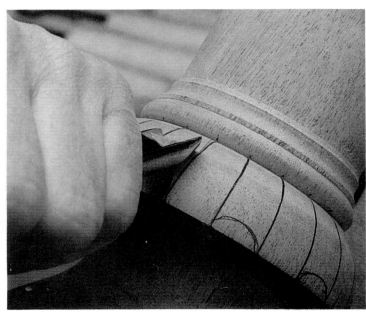

Starting part way up the concave segment, work your way up. By starting here you relieve the pressure on the wood and get a cleaner cut.

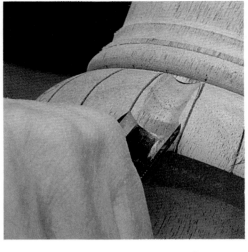

Widen the cut to the lines you drew.

Progress. The concave portion should appear to go under the bead.

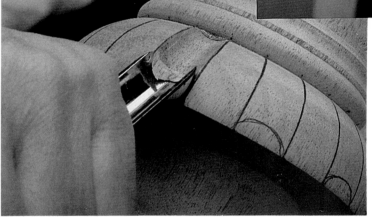

Continue to the bottom of the concave segment.

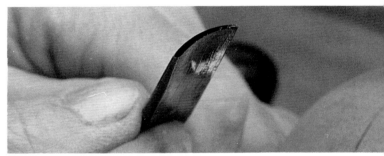

Next we round over the convex elements of the gadroon. I use a gouge with a slight curve to it for this. This is a 6/13.

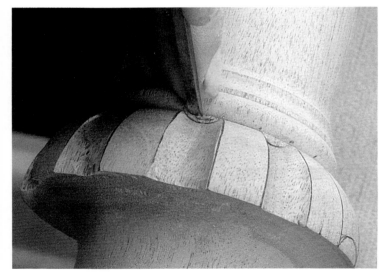

Where the gadroon meets the bead at the top of the segment, use a straight chisel to clean it up.

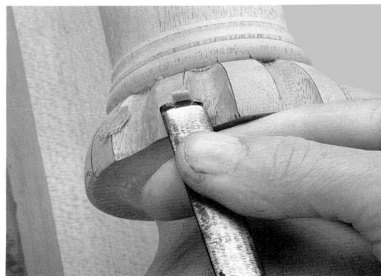

Keep the cup of the gouge against the wood.

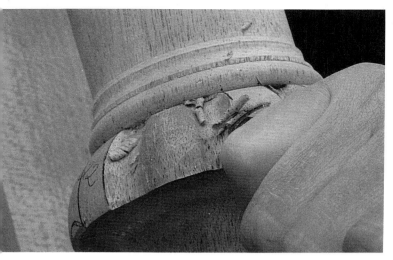

Work from one side of the segment...

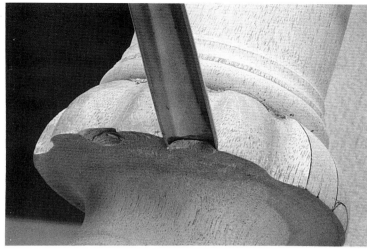

Establish the bottom edges of the concave segments by driving a gouge straight in.

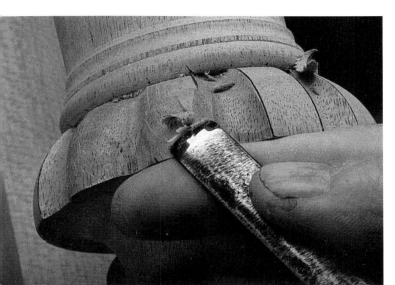

to the other, giving it a nice curved surface.

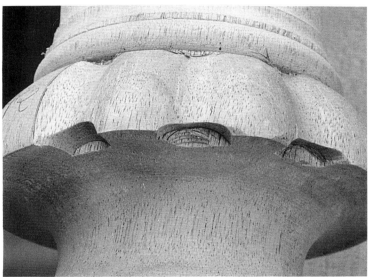

This is just establishing the line, and the cut does not need to go too deep.

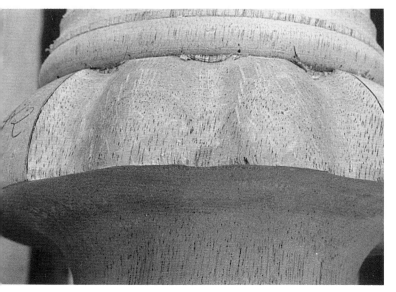

Progress. Continue all the way around.

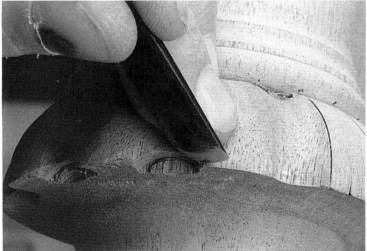

With the cup of the gouge against the piece, trim the corners of the convex segments to make their ends rounded and blended with the concave.

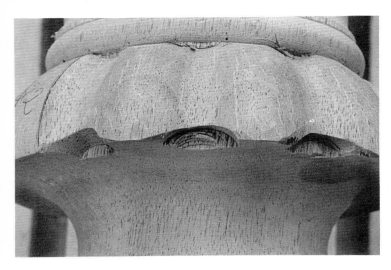

The result.

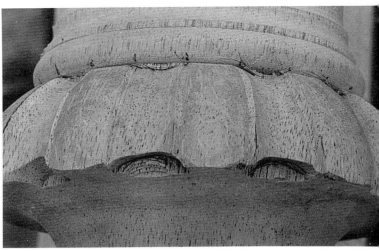

The result is a nice delineation of the segments.

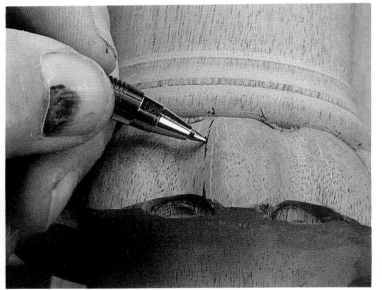

From the marking at the lathe, there are indications on the bead where the original lines were. We need to reestablish them on the gadroon. Mark at the bead and at the end of the collar, then connect the marks.

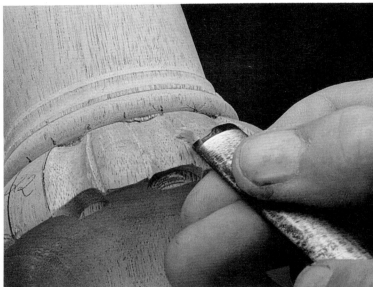

Round the convex segments over to the v-cuts. Try to make these segments uniformly round.

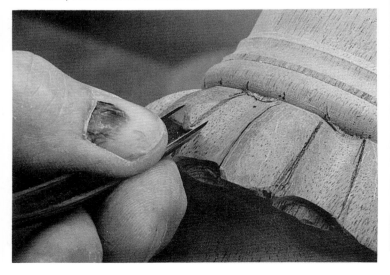

With a v-tool and constant pressure, follow these lines.

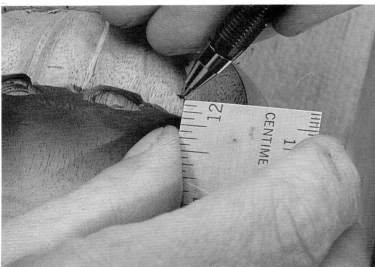

The decoration on each convex segment consists of a dot and a groove. The dot is 3/16" from the bottom of the segment.

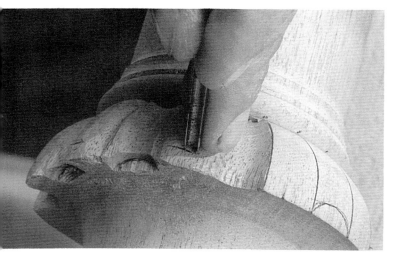

To create the dot we use a 6/3 gouge. We use it something like a drill bit. With the cup down, center it on the line and push straight in.

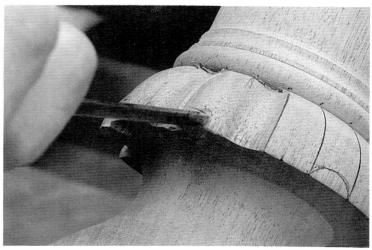

Gradually lower the angle of the gouge as you continue to go around...

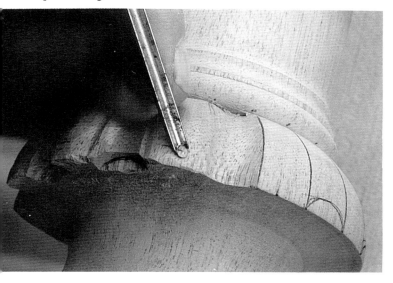

Rotate it around...

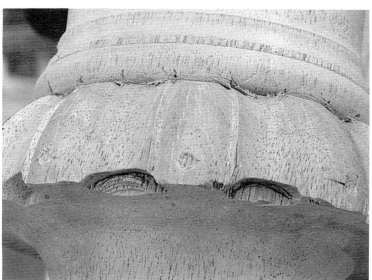

until the dot is lifted out.

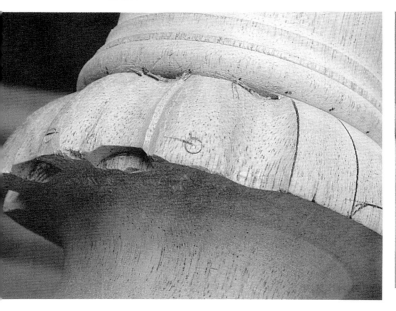

to create a circle.

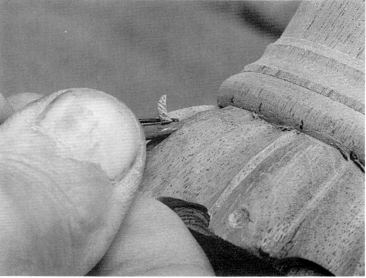

Next take an 11/2 veining gouge, and starting just above the dot run a vein up to the bead.

When this finished around the gadroon, the carving of it will be complete, except for light sanding.

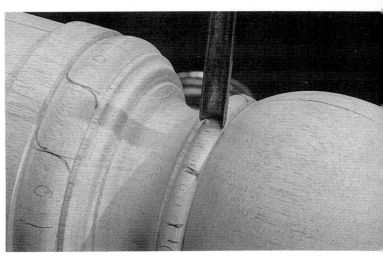

Continue with one side of the adjoining pearl...

Moving to the beading below the vase, drive the chisel straight in at one end of the lozenge...

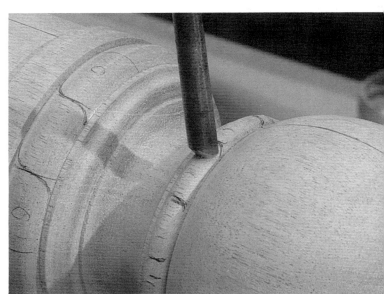

and the other.

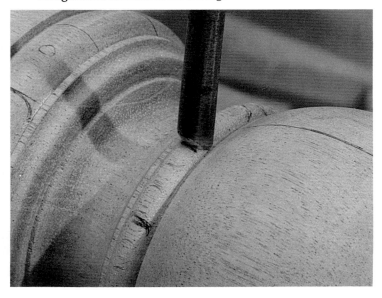

and at the other.

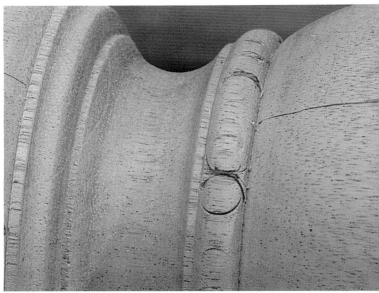

This will create a nice round pearl.

Continue with the other two pearls to get this result. Don't be too aggressive or you can chip the pearl off of the turning. The lozenge-three pearls-lozenge pattern will continue around the bead.

Pick away the material to be removed.

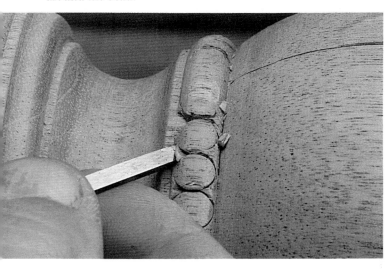

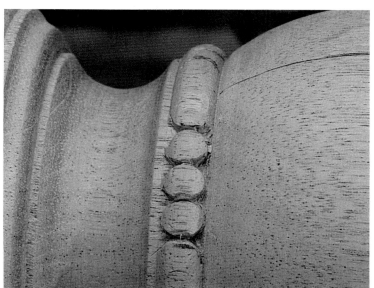

With a very small flat chisel, remove the corners between the pearls and lozenges. Continue around. The space at the bottom between the pearls and lozenges should be flush with the fillet below the bead.

Progress.

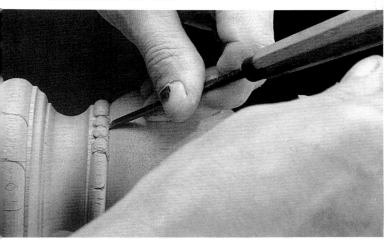

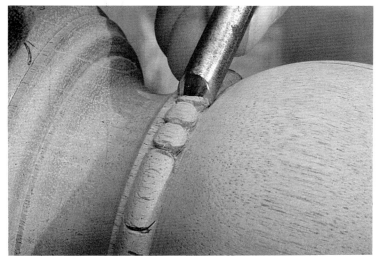

To get at the spaces above the pearls and lozenges, run your chisel into the space along the surface of the vase and tap. This must be a very light tap, or you will knock off a pearl.

Now we need to round the pearls up. The simplest way to do this is to use the same gouge you used to set their size. With the cup against the wood come over the top, giving the pearl its shape. Be careful not to take off too much.

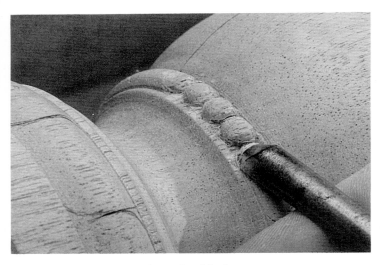

Do the same thing at the ends of the lozenges.

The result. This will continue around the bead.

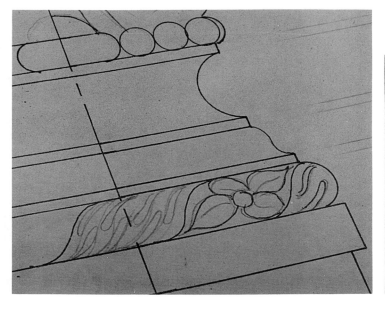

Refer to the rope and flower bead in the measured drawing.

Mark the center of the bead and reestablish the segment lines from earlier. In the center of alternating segments, draw a small circle which will be the middle of the flower.

The sweep of a gouge will create the curved line between the segments. It will go from the center to the edge in each direction. Find the one that fits (I'm using a 6/13 gouge). We lightly tap the chisel from the center mark to the edge of the bead, below...

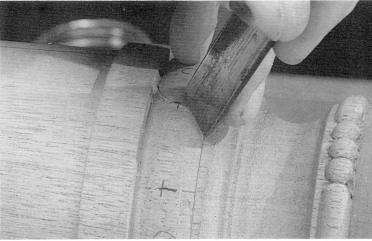

and above, reversing the chisel.

This creates a gentle S curve marking each segment. Continue all around the bead.

Draw the petals of the flowers to fill the spaces created.

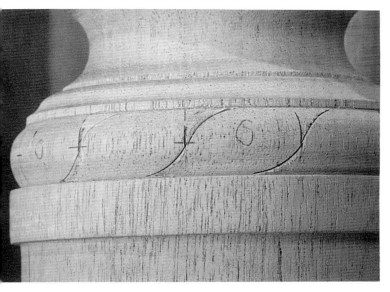

The result.

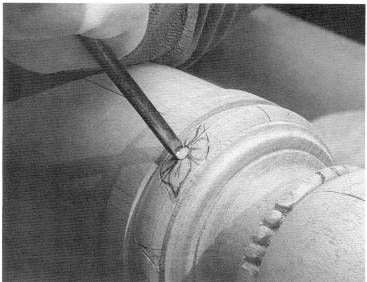

Drive the appropriately sized gouge lightly around the center of the flower.

Divide the flower in four sections.

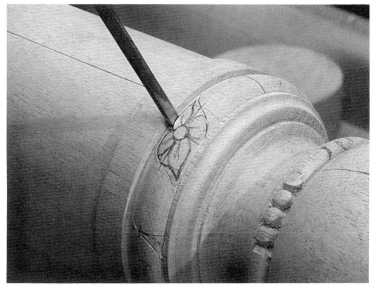

In the same way, define the outlines of the leaves.

With the outline established we need to set the ground around the flower.

The flower emerges as the background is taken away.

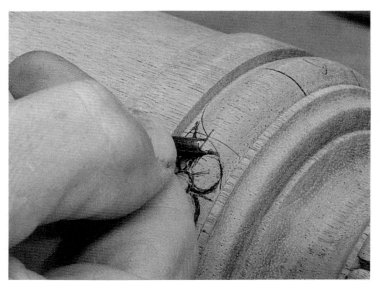

I'll use a small straight chisel (8/3) and a small gouge for this work (1/3). Use these tools to chip out around the flower.

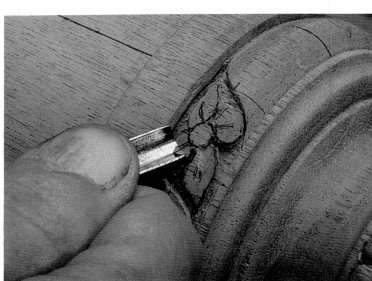

To shape the petals I begin by coming toward the center of the flower with a gouge.

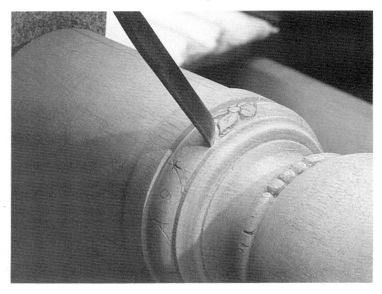

You may need to reset the S curves between the segments.

The result.

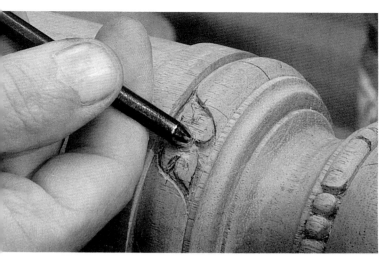

To round off the center, go over it with the cup of the chisel against it, as you did with the pearl on the bead.

Use the smallest veiner available to add veins to the petals.

Progress.

Finished except for some light touch-up.

Finish shaping the petals.

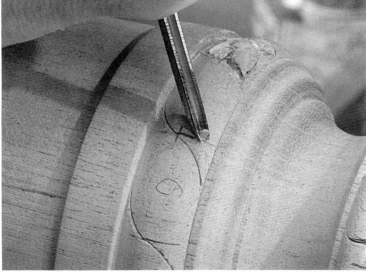

The rope is created by gouging a series of lines from the center line up...

like this.

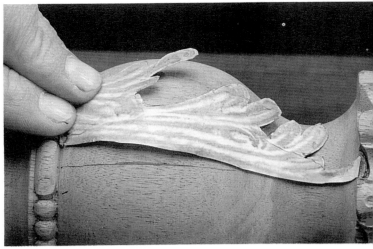

Lay the leaf pattern on the vase so that it meets the center line at the top.

Between these lines, create other lines going from the center to the bottom...

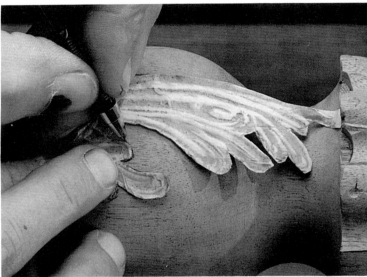

Draw the pattern, then turn it over and make its mirror image on the other side of the line. Repeat at the other two center lines.

This situates the element on the vase.

like this. The flower and the rope patterns alternate all the way around this bead.

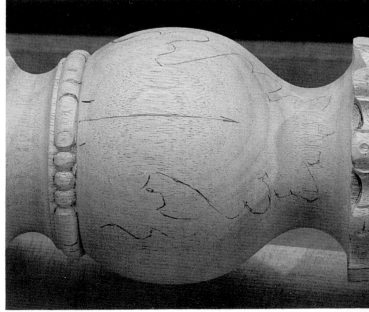

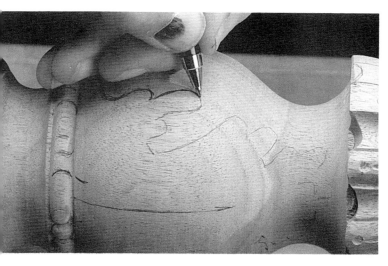

Referring to the drawing, go back and sharpen the outline.

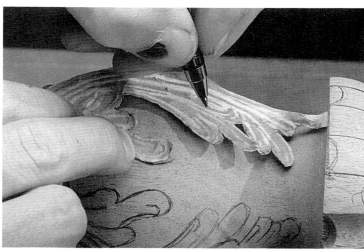

Continue with the pattern all around the vase.

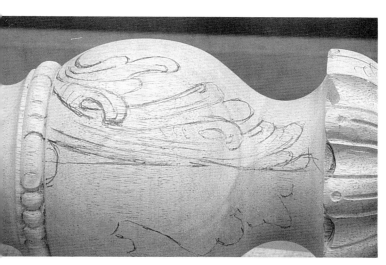

Add details as you go. Most of these will need to be done freehand, referring constantly to the drawing.

Copy the pattern in reverse to the other side of the center line.

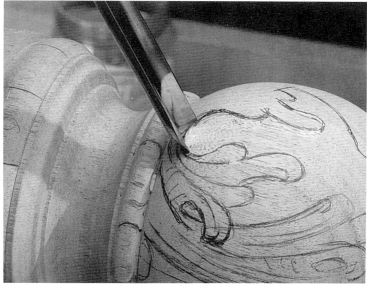

The carving of the pattern begins with establishing the outlines. For this process it is best to have a variety of gouges so you can match the sweep of a particular curve. Drive a gouge that matches the curve of an arc into the outline of the leaf, beginning where the two leaves meet.

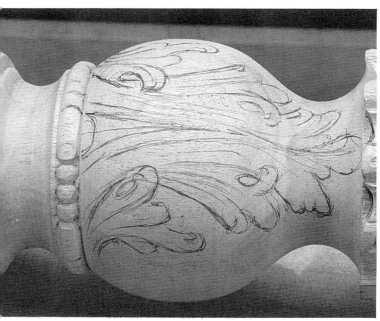

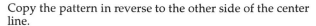

Continue the cut around to one side...

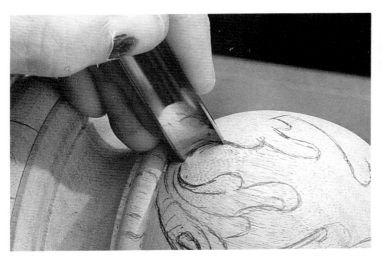

and the other.

Work all the way around the leaves, using gouges with matching sweeps to create the outline. This establishes the ground around the leaves.

By removing the shaded areas we raise the leaves from the surface of the vase.

Working out from the equator of the vase to avoid grain problems, use a fairly flat chisel to remove the wood from the ground. While I do this mostly by eye, the depth of the ground is approximately 1/8", though I don't go the whole way in one cutting.

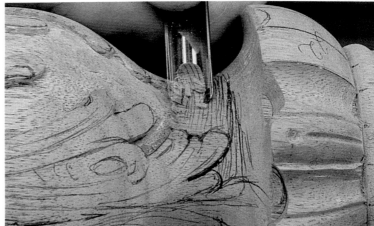

At the neck the grain makes it necessary to go across the it from side to side.

Come from the centers out to the sides.

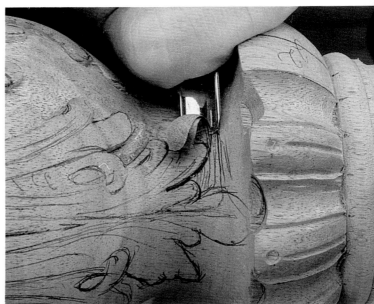

Undercut beneath the gadroon.

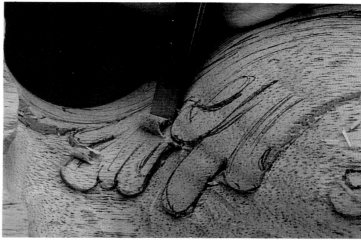

Relieve the wood around each of these overlapping fronds.

It should be something like this, with smoothing coming later.

As you can see from the pattern, two fronds on each side overlap the others giving a three dimensional look to the piece. Cut along their edges to define them.

There is a teardrop shaped section beside the each of the overlapping fronds, that is quite a deep space. Go straight in with your gouge...

then lower the angle of the chisel and clean out the space.

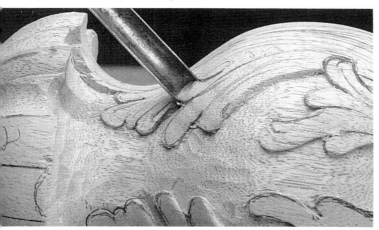

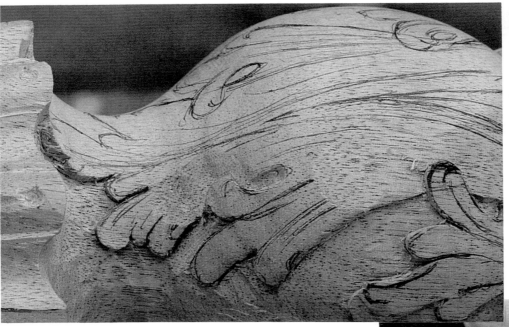

With the cup against the frond, cut straight in to shape its end.

The result.

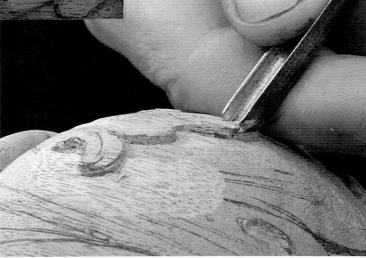

With a gouge, carve down the center of each frond to cup it. Working away from the high point of the ball will enable you to slice the grain.

With the gouge angle lowered come back at the end to clean it up.

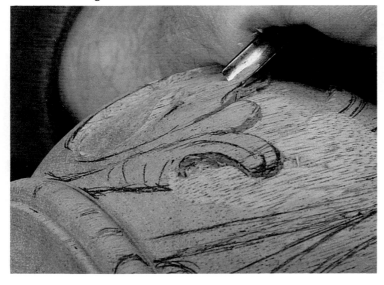

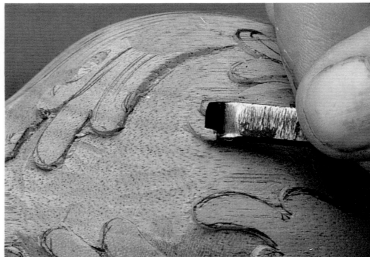

Continue on each of the regularly shaped fronds.

With the shape defined, round the end of the frond with a straight chisel.

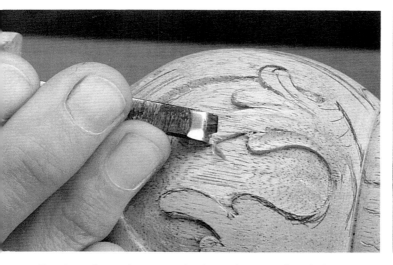

Continue down the exposed sides. Where one frond abuts another there will be a ridge, so don't go too far.

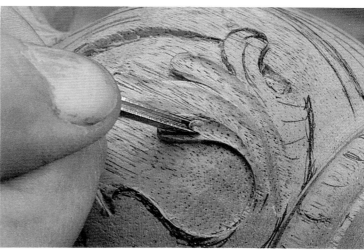

When the frond is cupped go down the center with a veiner and carve a central vein.

Progress.

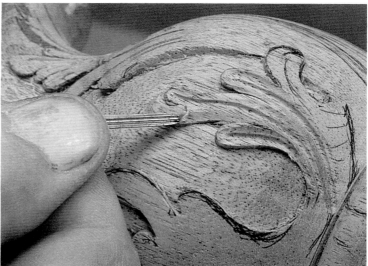

Some fronds, like this one, are slightly turned, presenting an s-shaped profile. The vein line should follow the curve and be slightly off-center. You can see the result in the next photo.

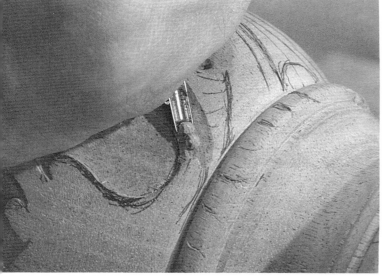

Continue the cupping of the frond into the bridge with the next leaf.

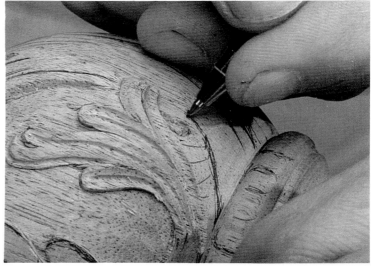

Remark the lines that you removed earlier.

Progress. Work continues in much the same way until the foliage is complete.

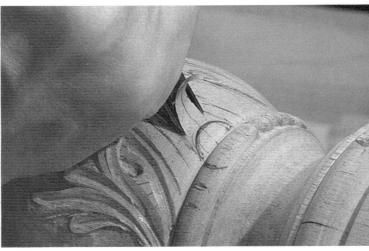

Come back to the circle...

Between the two halves of a leaf, at the bead, there is a semi-circle. Choose a gouge that bridges the two sides of the leaf and push straight in to form this circle.

use the gouge to go deeper...

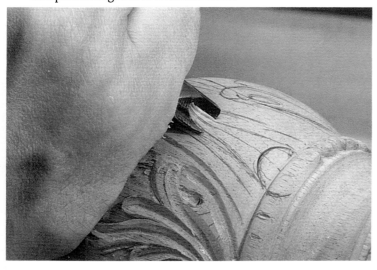

With a smaller gouge, come back to the semi-circle starting at the point of the triangle formed by the two halves.

then move to a smaller gouge and deepen the triangle.

Clean up around the semi-circle, using the small chisel to get in the corners...

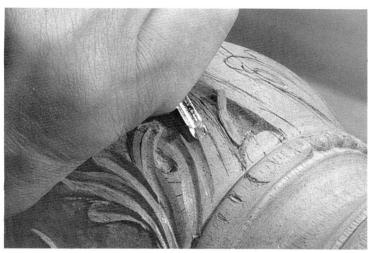

With a small gouge establish the lines along the center of the foliage.

and a larger gouge to clean the general shape.

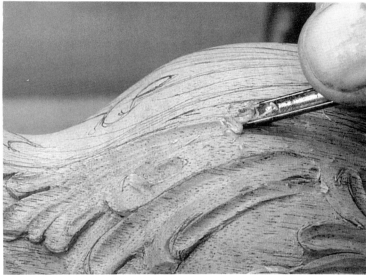

Remember to change directions so you are slicing the grain and not cutting into it. Work away from the widest point of the vase bulb. Blend these lines in with the fronds.

Progress.

Go back and make adjustments, making some of the fronds deeper than the others.

The basic modelling is complete. Now it needs to be repeated on the mirror side.

The result.

As you can see on the pattern, some of the stalks have a notched detail that is created by making a stop with the gouge straight in...

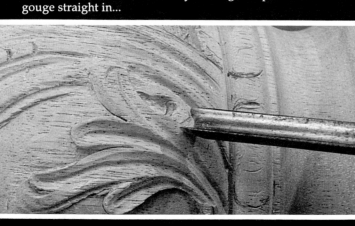

Go back and smooth the background. This may take longer than the leaves, but it is important if the leaves are to appear to grow on the vase.

and coming back to it.

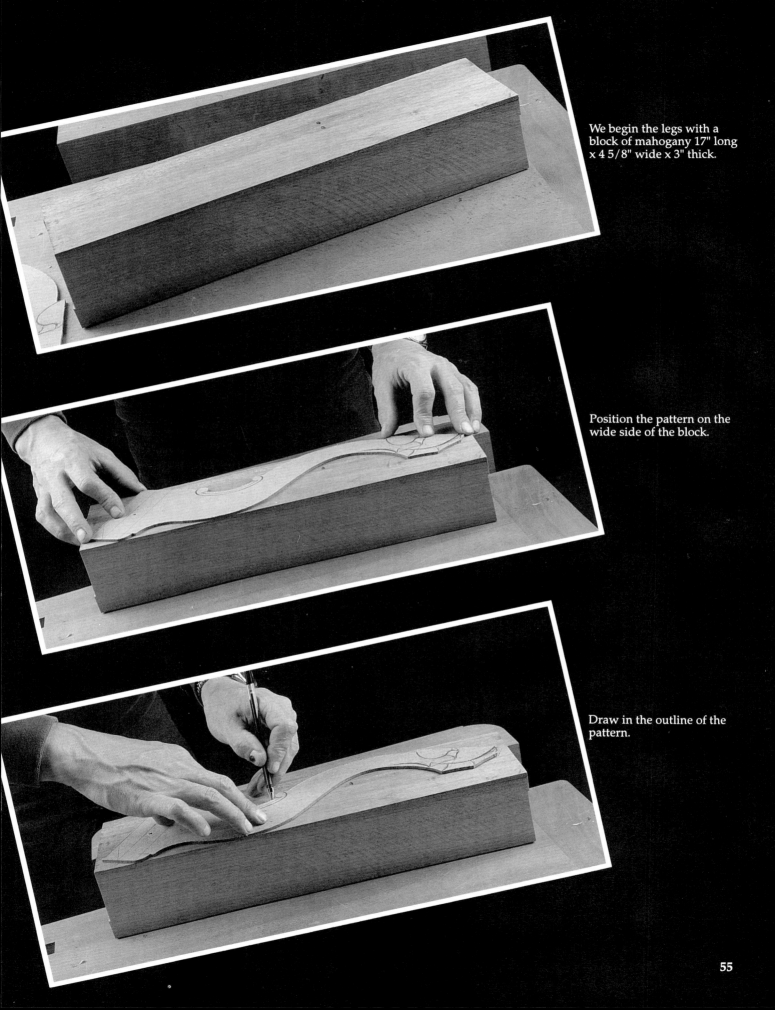

We begin the legs with a block of mahogany 17" long x 4 5/8" wide x 3" thick.

Position the pattern on the wide side of the block.

Draw in the outline of the pattern.

55

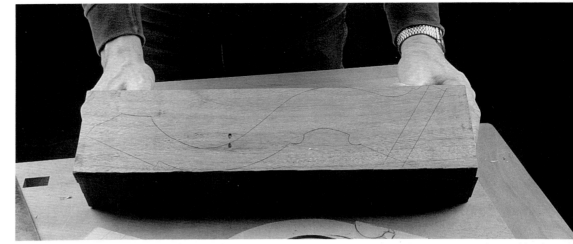

The result.

Cut the pattern out on the bandsaw.

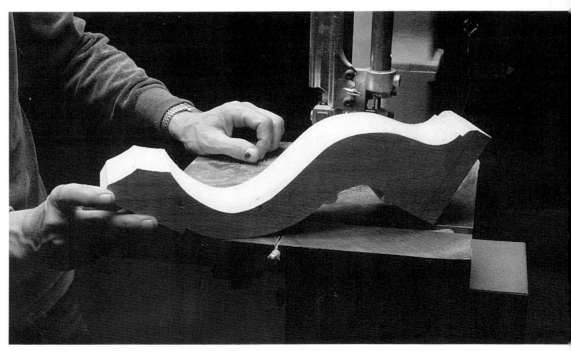

The result.

Find the center.

The tapering pattern is cut from aluminum flashing. This is bendable and conforms to the shape of the leg very well.

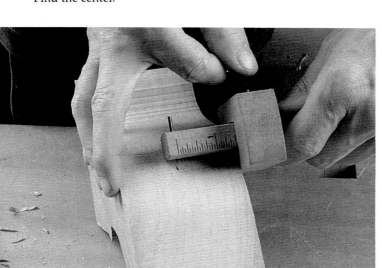

Set the marking gauge to the center mark.

The bend at the end so it fits the notch at the top of the leg.

Use the marking gauge to carry the center line all around the leg. This center line is important for several reasons. We will be using it to line up the dovetailing, the carving patterns, and also to lay the tapering pattern.

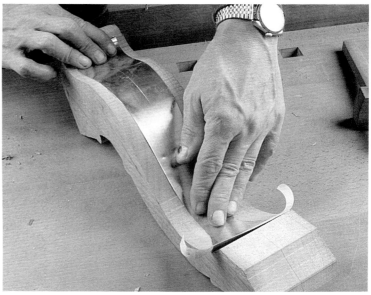

Lay the pattern along the center line.

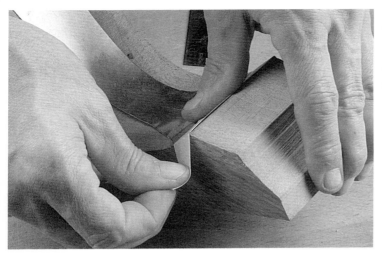

Tape down the foot end.

Mark the area to be cut away.

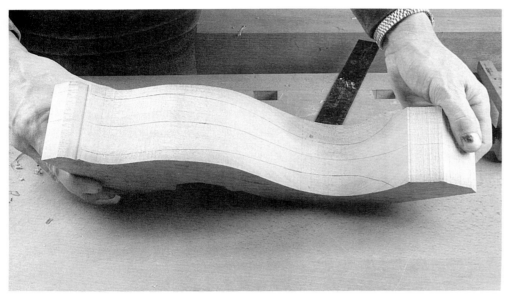

Draw the outline.

Move to the bandsaw and start cutting at the foot. At the beginning of the cut the foot is flat to the table.

We need to add material from the top of the leg to the foot. At the top of the leg we need to measure from the outside to the line of the leg and carry it around the back. When I bandsaw on these lines, I will have a nice flat piece for joining to the foot.

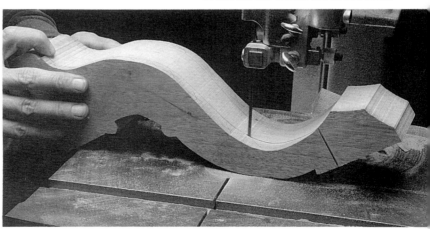

As you move back past the foot the leg should be tilted back so the bottom of the shoulder rests on the table.

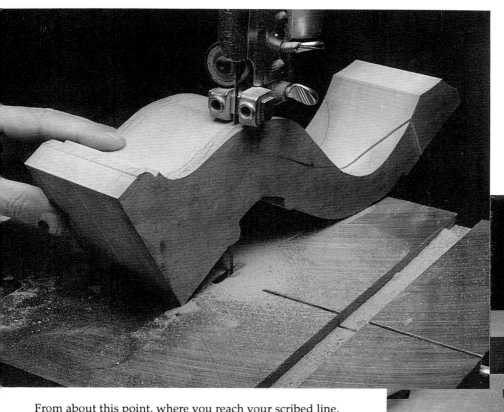

From about this point, where you reach your scribed line, keep the cut nice and straight.

The leg cut out.

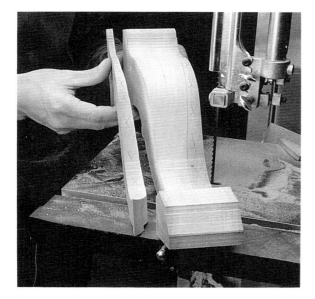

The result. Repeat on the other side of the leg.

You can see the scribe marks at the back end of the leg. You want to try to leave enough wood on the outside of the scribe lines so you can dress the square later.

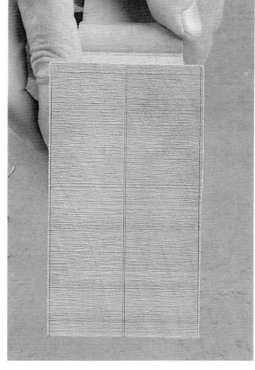

The result. Return to the bandsaw and cut it out.

To widen the foot we need to add 3/8" to each side. As we said this should come from the waste at the shoulder of the leg. If however these waste pieces end up too thin (as they did for us) don't despair. The piece you cut from the outline of the leg will work nicely. Scribe a mark on each side that is just a tad bit more than 3/8".

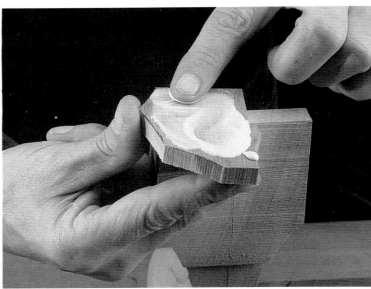

Cut it on the bandsaw, to the wide side of the line.

Spread glue on the surfaces, doing both additions at the same time.

Whichever way you get this extra piece, hold it against the leg and trace the outline of the foot.

Apply to each side of the foot and clamp in place.

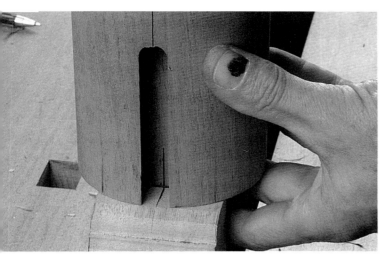

While the foot is setting up, I'll align the dovetail. Hold the pedestal on the top of the leg so the back of the dovetail mortise is even with the edge of the shoulder, and the center lines align.

Mark the shape of the pedestal on the top of the leg...

and mark the shape of the dovetail mortise.

The result.

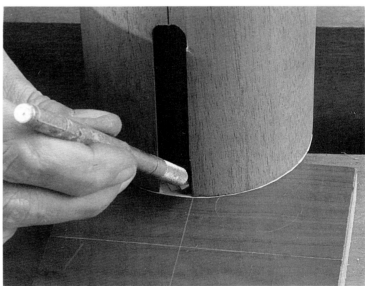

Cut a paper template to fit the base of the pedestal exactly. Cut out the dovetail mortises with knife to get an accurate pattern of the base of the pedestal. Because this determines the fit of the leg into the pedestal, it is important that it be as accurate as you can make it.

From our first fitting we found the distance of the shoulder. Set the marking gauge to this distance (approximately 5/16").

Mark both sides to establish the shoulders of the leg.

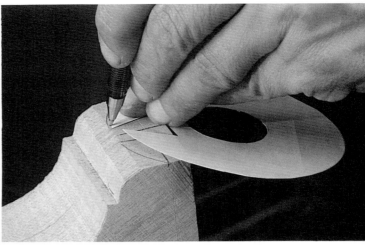

Make any corrections from your original lines.

Mark the shoulder on the top of the edge.

Draw a line from the point of the dovetail to the outside point.

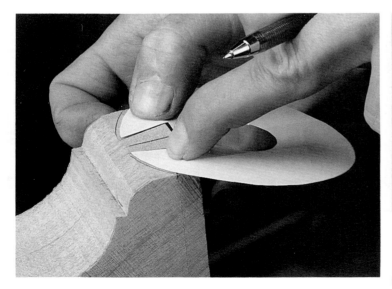

With the dovetail centers aligned, lay your pattern so the edges come to the marks on the side.

This is the saw line.

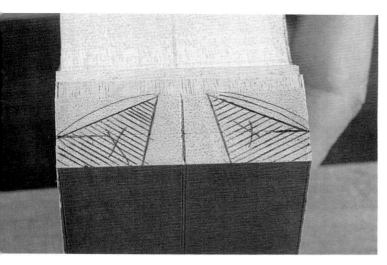

These darkened areas will be sawed away.

Ready for sawing.

With the marking gauge carry the lines of the dovetail down the back of the leg.

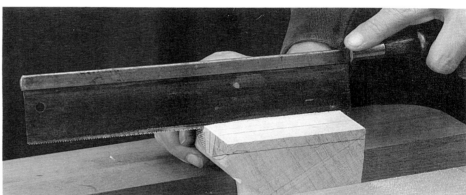

You can either saw this on the table saw or by hand. Carefully follow the line of the dovetail...

Mark the pattern out on the bottom of the leg as well.

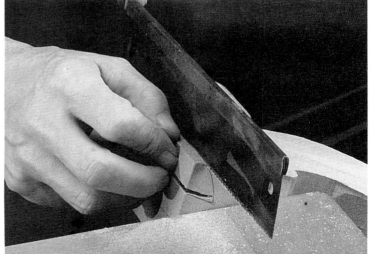

Then come back to it from the side.

The result. Repeat on the other side.

Later we will remove the wood defined by the curve the pedestal. It is darkened in this photo.

When hand sawing it is important to establish a perfectly straight line. To do this I begin by cutting perpendicular to the surface.

To begin laying out the foot we establish a circle that is 3" in diameter. Lay the pattern on the foot and carry the center mark to the sole of the foot.

Bring the line across the foot.

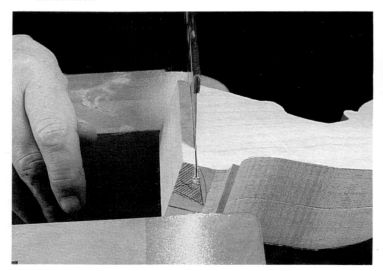

When a straight trough is established I angle the piece in the vise, so that I cut straight down.

64

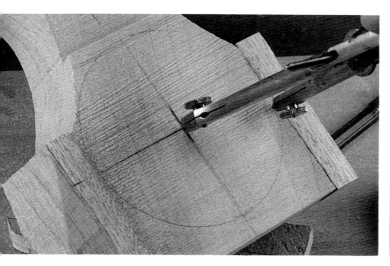

Where it crosses the median line, lay the point of a compass set at 1 1/2" and strike a 3" circle.

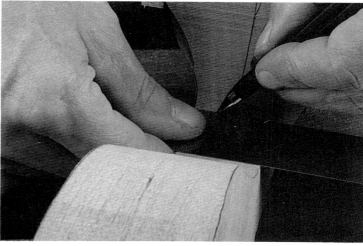

and up into the ankle.

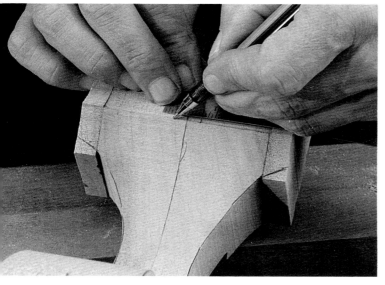

To establish the center toe, start at the top of the foot at the center line, and mark 1/4" to each side.

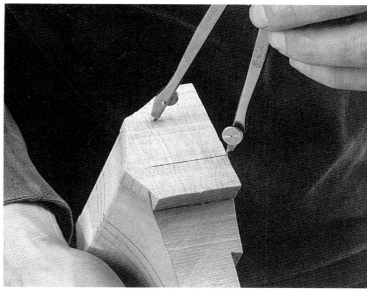

From the point where the side center line meets the sole, scribe a 1 1/2" circle on the profile of the foot..

Carry the lines down the front of the foot...

Mark 1/4" on each side of the center line to establish the side toes.

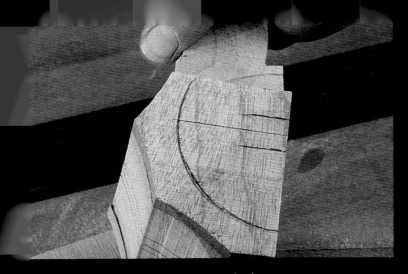

Carry the lines about halfway up the foot.

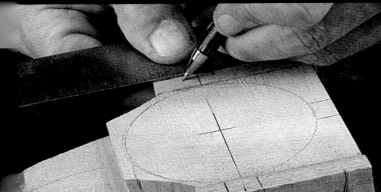

Carry the toe lines around to the bottom of the foot.

By holding the sole against the bandsaw table you can rough out the shape of the foot. Be sure to leave some extra around the outline.

I carry the toe lines all around the foot to help me see the wood to be removed around the ball. This will enable us to

This is a hard foot to carve, and these stages must be gone through one-by-one. The bandsawing will take you to about

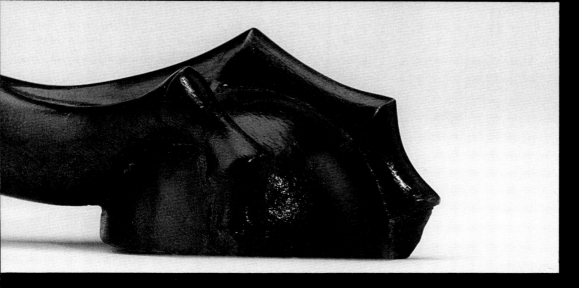

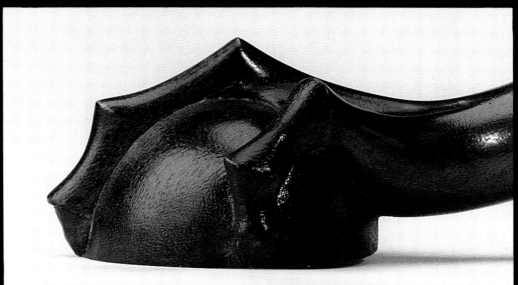

Full-sized photographs of the foot.

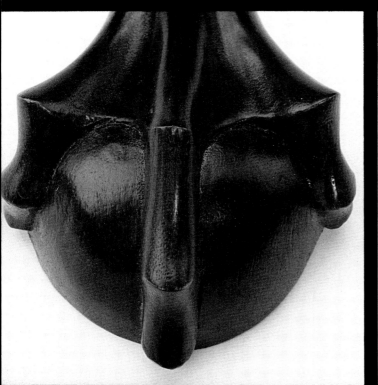

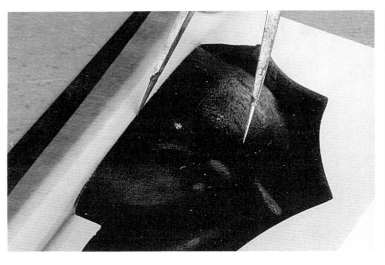

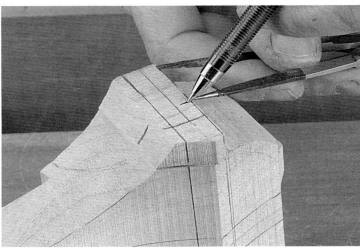

Using the full-sized picture and calipers measure from the bottom of the foot to the inside of the side knuckle.

and transfer it. You will continue to do this for all the knuckles of the foot.

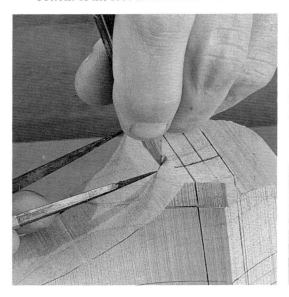

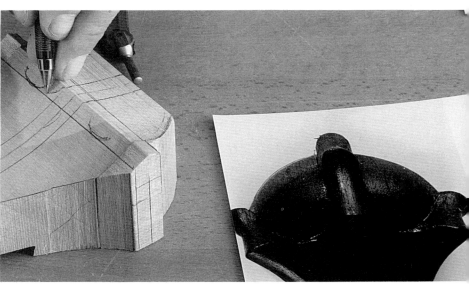

Transfer it to the piece of wood.

Refer to the top view photo and draw the webbing between the toes. These marks will be carved away, and are, in fact, only a close approximation. We need to have an idea of where things are before we start carving the foot.

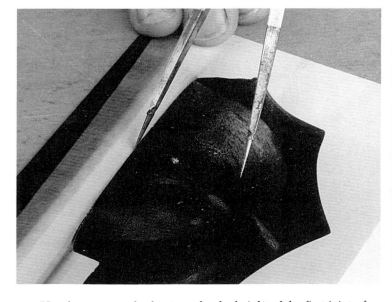

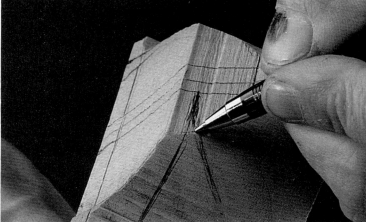

Use the same method to transfer the height of the first joint of the side knuckle...

Carry the 1 1/2" mark around from the side to the front. Using the full sized photos as a guide, start where that line meets the center and draw in the ball. Repeat on all sides.

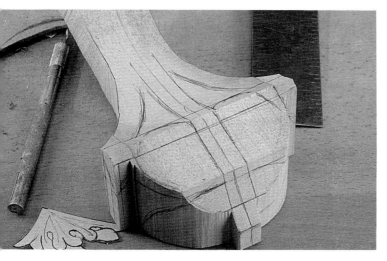

When all the guidelines are drawn, we begin removing stock from the ball.

With a 1/2" flat chisel I begin to shape the ball by cutting back to the saw cut from the outside of the foot.

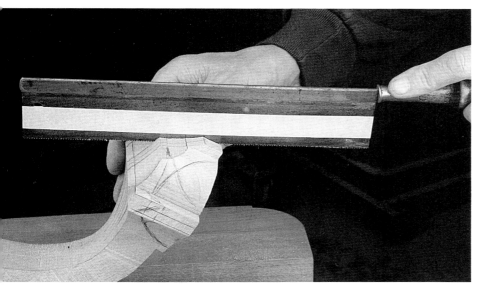

Begin with some straight saw cuts to delineate the middle toe. We want to go about 3/8" deep, so I make a tape mark on the saw to tell me when to stop. Keep the saw parallel to the facets of the toes.

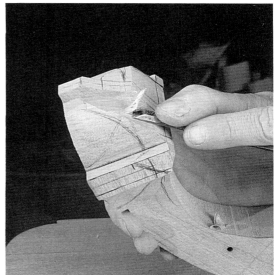

After it is started you may switch and go down the foot.

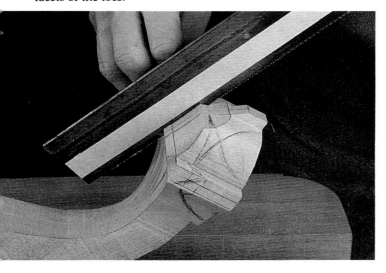

Continue beside each segment of the center toe.

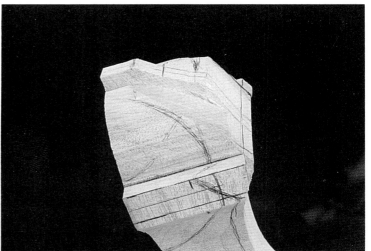

Take it to this point and repeat on the other side. You want to try to do everything equally on both sides as you are progressing.

Remove the waste above the side toes.

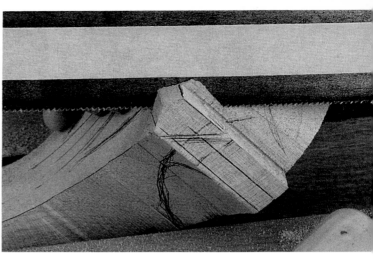

Cut straight down beside the ball, taking off the excess at the top of the side toe.

The grain switches here so I need to cut back toward the middle.

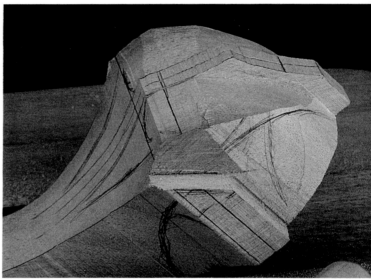

The result.

The foot is beginning to take shape.

Returning to the side toe, cut a stop in its top line, about 1/2" deep. Repeat on the other side. This is not final layout, but only rough stock removal. It must be done step by step or you will run into trouble later.

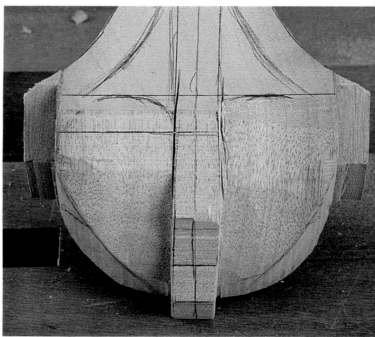

Round the top of the ball...

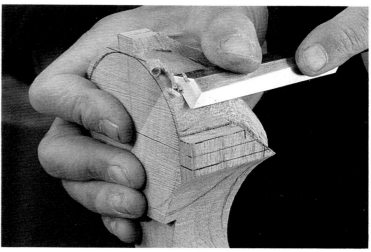

Work your way to the bottom. There is a circle on the bottom that is the final circumference of the ball. During the roughing stage come no closer to it than 1/16".

To about this state. Repeat on the other side.

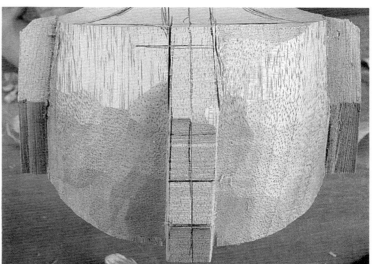

The ball is starting to emerge.

Continue rounding the facets off.

Reestablish the height of the ball, carrying the line around.

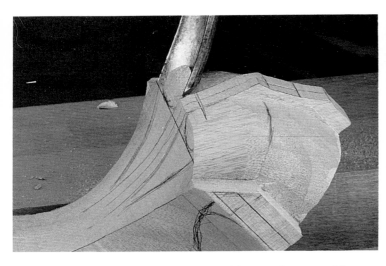

With a carving gouge relieve some of the wood on top of the ball between the toes. This is a No. 17 25mm bent gouge, but a straight gouge could be used as well.

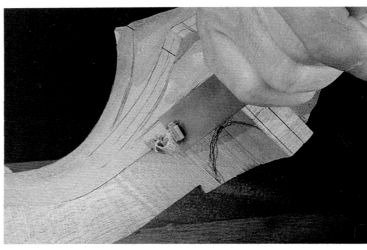

To get a better feel for the shape and position of the outside toes, I'm going to round their upper edges, where they go up to the ankle.

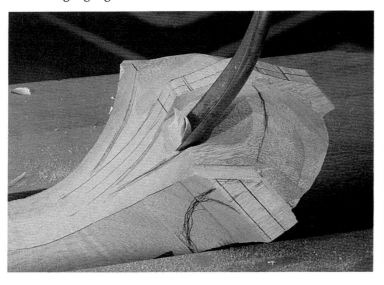

Switch to a smaller gouge (8/18) to get up into the narrower area.

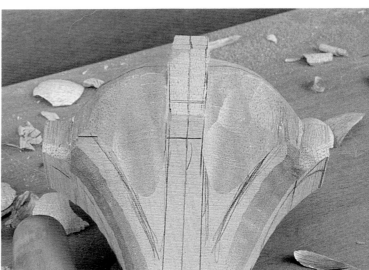

Progress. At this time it might be a good idea to round the ankle.

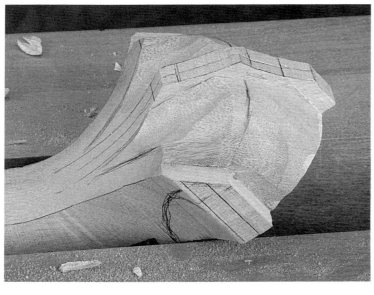

This will take you to about this point.

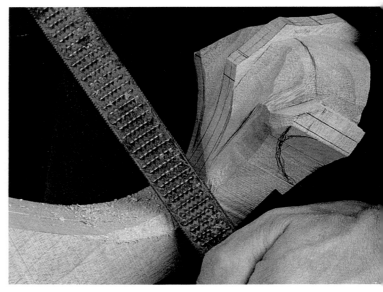

To do this I begin with a very coarse rasp.

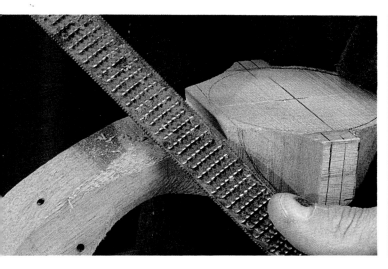

Continue around the bottom. The ankle at this point is practically round, point D on the drawing.

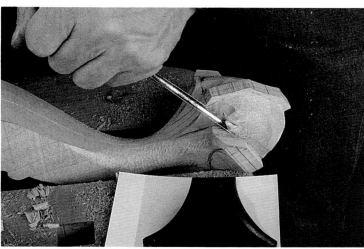

With a small gouge, follow the line of the webbing.

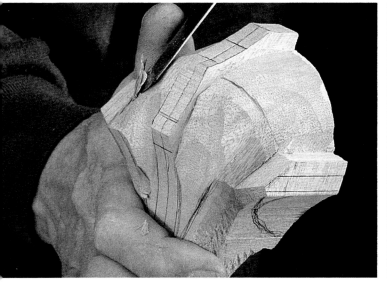

That done we return to the process of rounding the ball.

The result. Repeat on the other side.

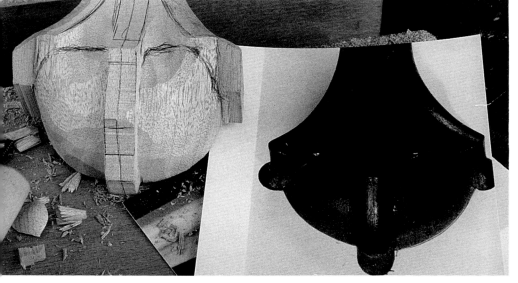

Referring to the full-sized photo again, draw in the line of the webbing.

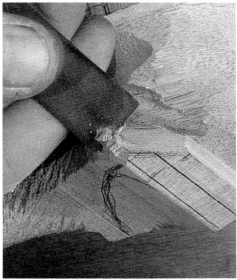

Round the side toes.

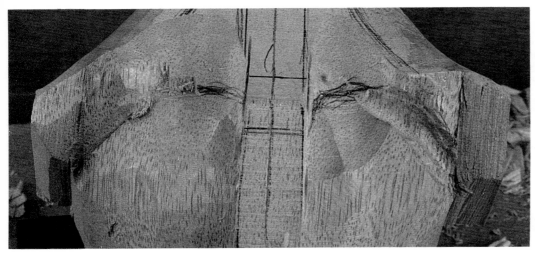

This begins to get the shape of the toe.

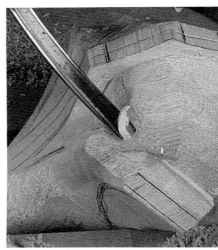

With a parting tool go down the inside of the knuckle.

Establish the line of the web by driving a gouge into it that matches its sweep..

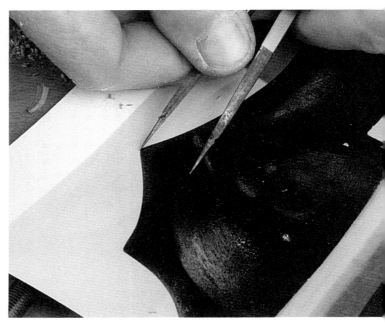

Use the full size photo and the caliper to check the height of the center toe at each knuckle and the center of the valley between. At this point in the process you will need to rely on the photographs to continue the process.

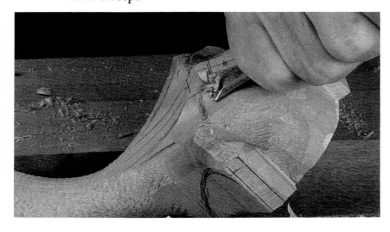

Cut back to the line along the surface of the ball. Before moving to the next step, repeat the process on the other side.

You can see we have some distance to go.

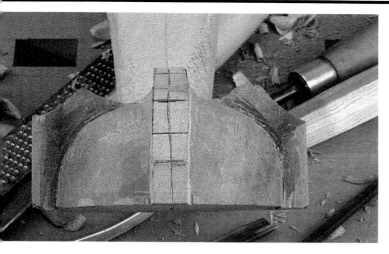 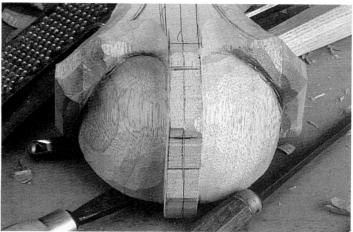

Carve the ball until it is to shape. While it is not yet to its final dimension, it is starting to look like a ball.

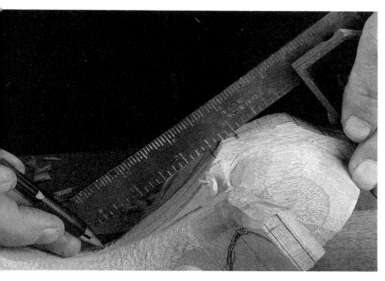 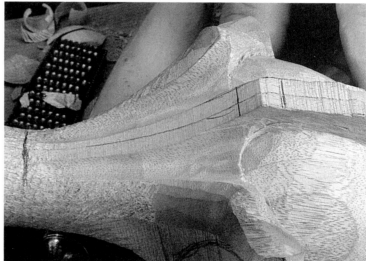

Now we relieve the wood between the toes in the webbed area. With a square, measure 4 1/2" from the end of the foot and make a mark on the ankle. This is the end of the webbing.

Carve it to this point...

 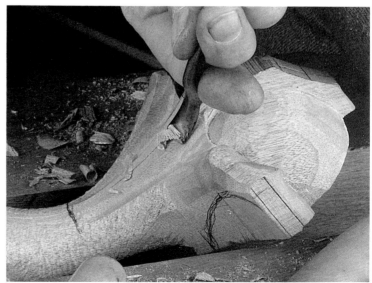

With a gouge take the webbing back to the mark.

then round the toes into the troughs. Don't go to the finished size yet. I'm using a back bent gouge.

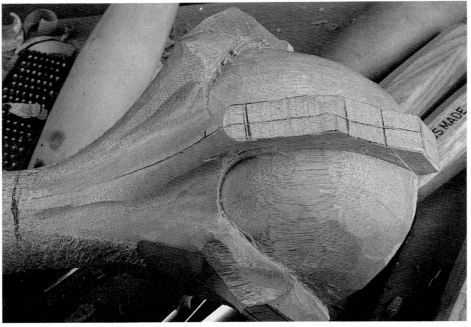

Progress.

Slice back to the line from the ball.

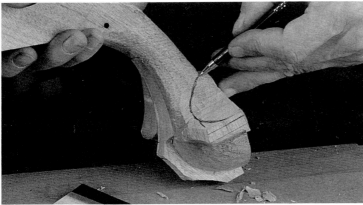

Referring to the full-sized photo, draw in the area behind and under the back toes.

Set the lines by driving chisels with matching sweeps into them.

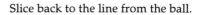

Continue deepening the area until the outside toe is established. Now all we need to do is round the ball under the toe and shape the ankle into the ball.

Carry the shaping around the back of the foot.

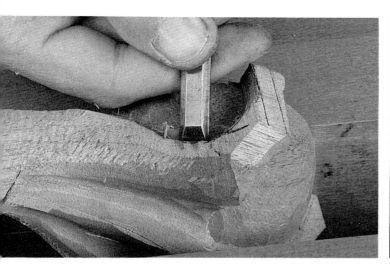

When the basic shape is set, go back and carry the surface of the ball under the toe.

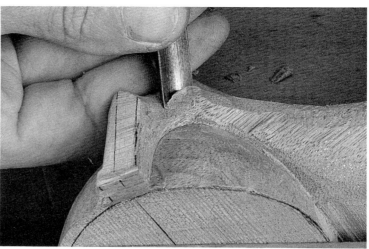

To trim the back side of the toe toward the ball I use a gouge and cut like this.

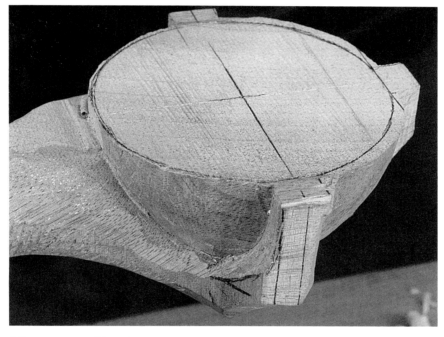

After we get to this point we need to define the toe.

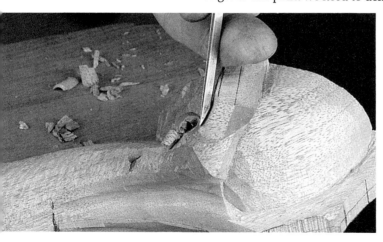

Begin by rounding off the toe. The grain switches direction relative to your cut, so you need to continually switch the piece around so you are cutting in the correct direction.

Continue with the lower segment of the toe.

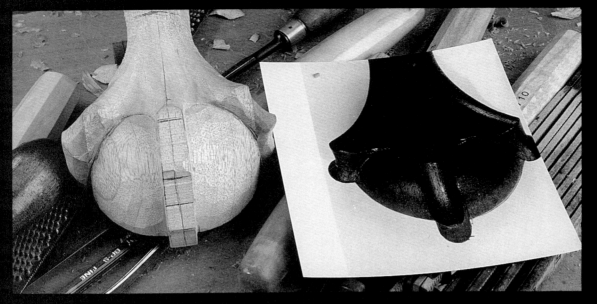

At this point check the carving with the full-sized photo for position and shape. Make adjustments as necessary.

The basic shape of the back toes is established. The foot is now 90% carved. The rest of the work is fine tuning.

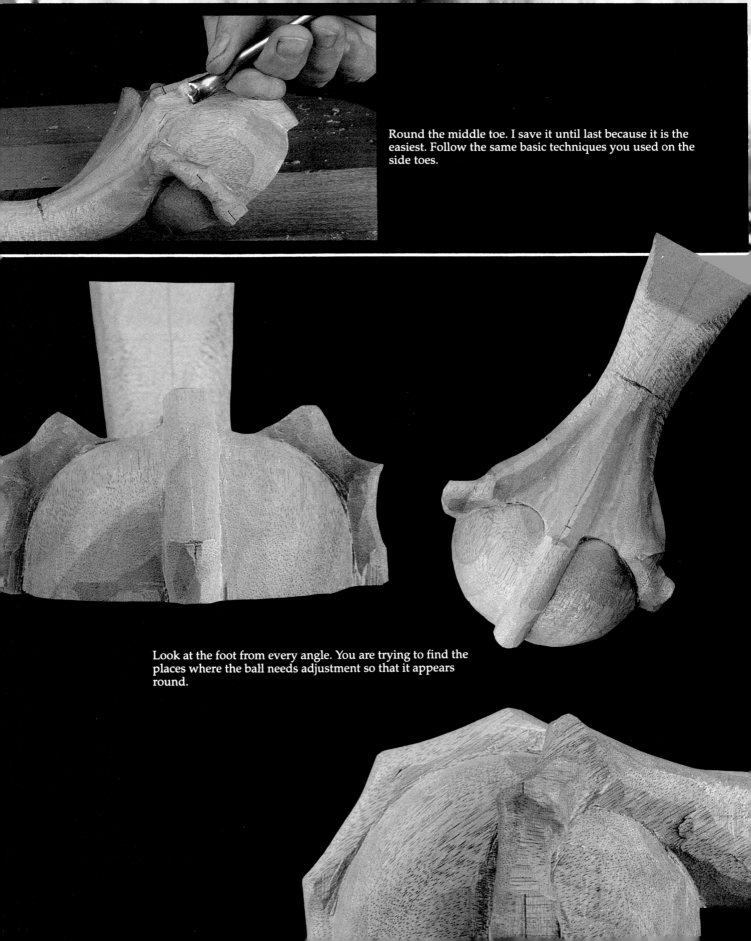

Round the middle toe. I save it until last because it is the easiest. Follow the same basic techniques you used on the side toes.

Look at the foot from every angle. You are trying to find the places where the ball needs adjustment so that it appears round.

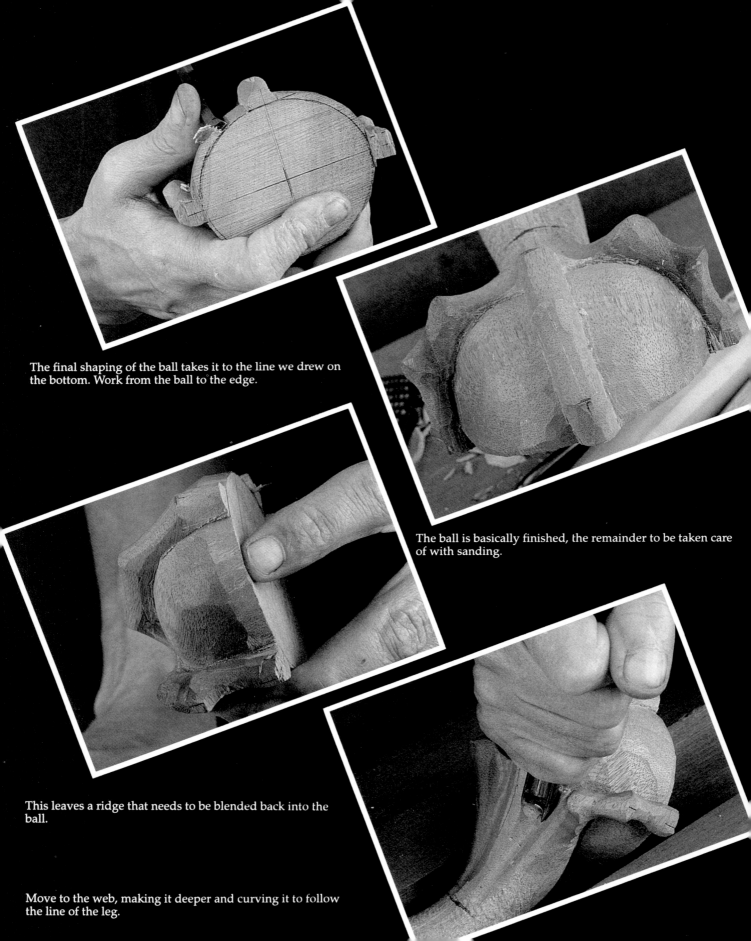

The final shaping of the ball takes it to the line we drew on the bottom. Work from the ball to the edge.

The ball is basically finished, the remainder to be taken care of with sanding.

This leaves a ridge that needs to be blended back into the ball.

Move to the web, making it deeper and curving it to follow the line of the leg.

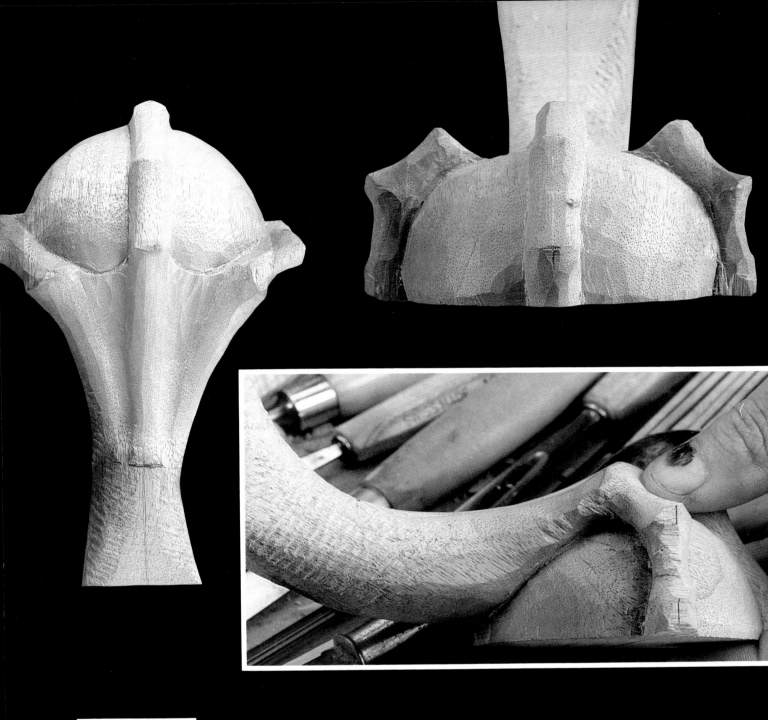

Progress.

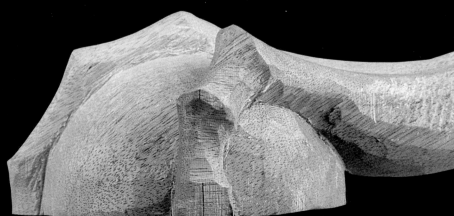

Shape the area beside the dovetail so it will fit against the pedestal. If you remember we marked it earlier. Clean it out with a gouge with a slight sweep, and cut from the bottom of the leg to the top. This slices across the grain instead of into it. This can be tough going so be patient.

Work your way up.

The goal is to achieve a smooth, straight curve that will fit snugly against the curve of the pedestal.

Pare the dovetail down for an exact fit.

The elements of the leg will have the same arc as the pedestal. Mark the curves so they are parallel.

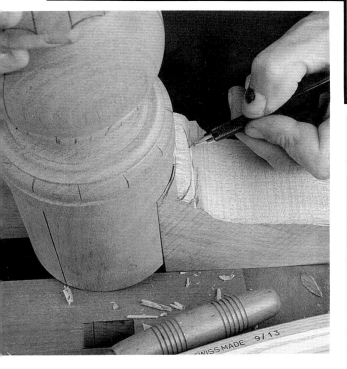

Test fit the leg. There is a little gap on this side that will need adjustment by a slight trimming of the dovetail.

Make a saw cut at the return on the corner. This will act as a stop....

as you cut back to it with a chisel.

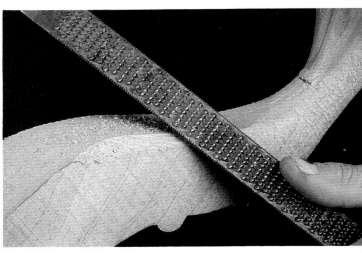

Rough shape the leg with the rasp.

With the chisel, continue knocking off the corner onto the shoulder.

Establish the round decoration on the underside of the leg by driving a matching-sized chisel into it. This will help protect against you rasping it away!

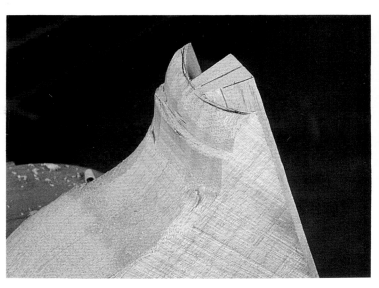

This gives the start of a curve in the upper elements.

Trim back to the stop with a chisel before returning to the rasp.

The rasping takes the leg to roughly an octagonal shape, having knocked off the corners.

Switch to a spokeshave and round the leg. I begin at about mid-knee.

Switching to a smaller spokeshave makes the ankle go more easily.

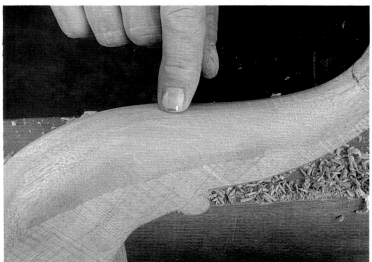

Remember when we scribed a middle line down the leg? While shaving the leg, try to leave at least a hint of it. This will be very useful when we begin to lay the carving patterns.

I often switch to a flat chisel for some of the this rounding. Just feels more comfortable somehow. Continue to round the upper portion of the leg.

Where the grains change direction, like here, use a sharp gouge and go across the grain.

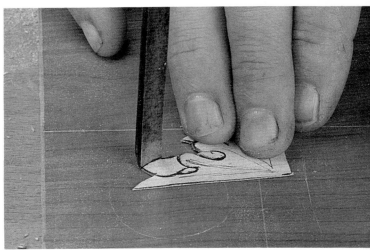

Copy the pattern from the book and trim it using chisels that match the pattern's sweeps and curves. These are the same chisels you will use to set the pattern on the leg.

Clean up the marks from the band saw with a low angle block plane.

The smaller carving will be done with #10 gouges with various widths, and #11 veiners.

A fine flat file helps take away some bumps and lumps and prepare the surface for carving.

The longer curves will be cut with flatter gouges, mostly #8 & #9, ranging in width from 3mm to 11mm.

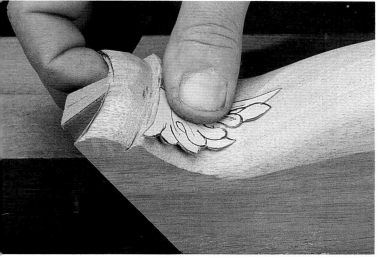

Align the top leaf pattern with the center line

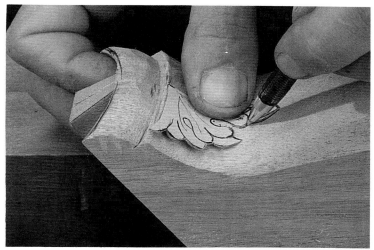

and draw its outline.

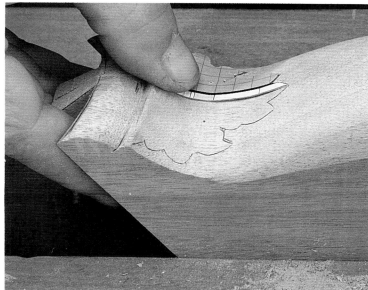

Turn the pattern over and draw the other side.

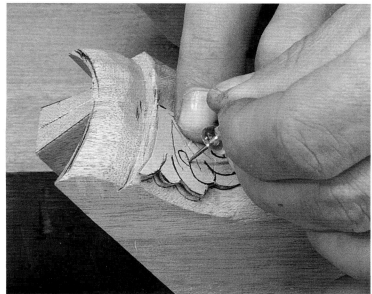

Use a pin to mark the round relief areas in the leaf pattern.

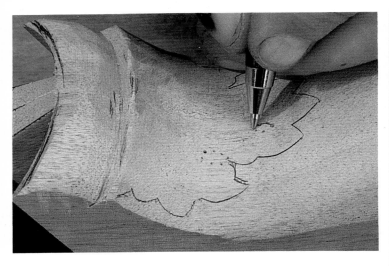

Connect the dots.

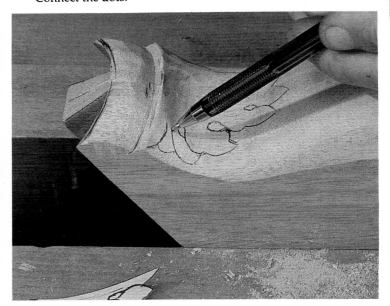

Referring to the patter, draw in the rest of the detail.

Repeat on the other side. The darkened loops will be relieved to the surface of the leg.

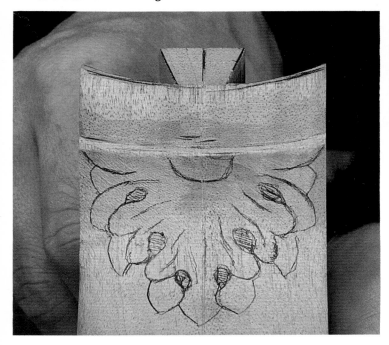

The drawings will make it clear which patterns overlap which. Keep it handy for reference. Select your first gouge and work your way around the leaf, setting all the lines that match the sweep of the gouge. With the gouge going straight tap it lightly one or two times to set the lines. Here at the edge there is a danger of chipping, so go lightly and be careful.

Switch to the next gouge and follow the same procedure. This is a smaller flatter gouge. Continue in the same until the outline of every part of the leaf is established.

A small gouge will do the small curves quite nicely.

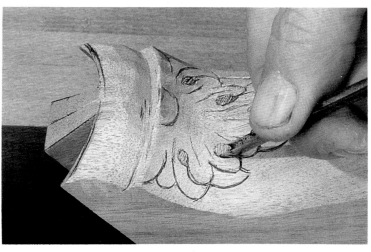

Come from the other end with the same gouge and clean out the loop.

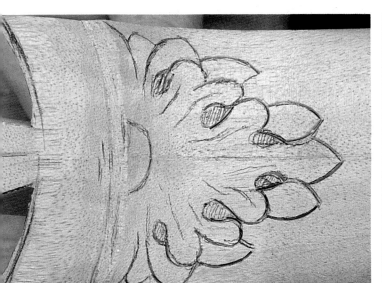

The outlines complete. You can see that the ends of the darkened loops are not outline. These will be cut next.

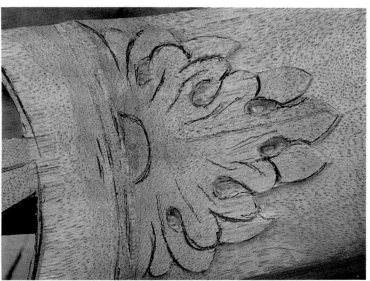

Do all the loops for this result.

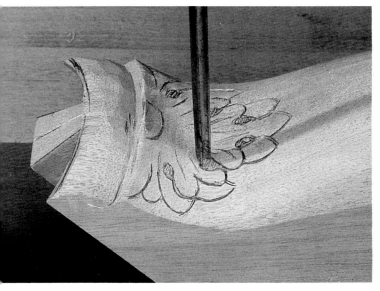

Drive the gouge straight in at the top of the loop.

Remove the ground around the leaves. Good control will keep you from cutting away a leaf!

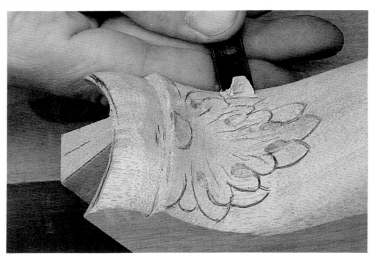

When the grain runs out you may need to come across it with an appropriate chisel. Again be careful not to cut into the leaf itself.

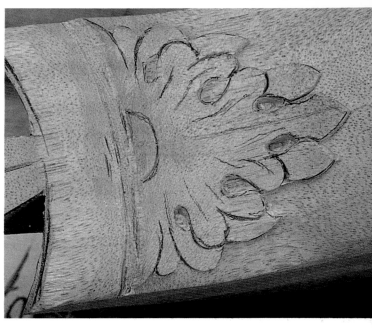

The foliage is set in.

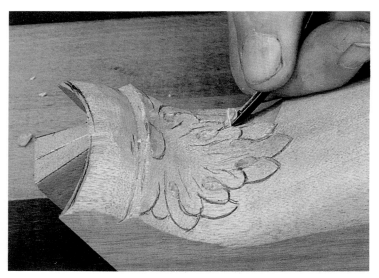

A small bent gouge is good for getting into a tight spot.

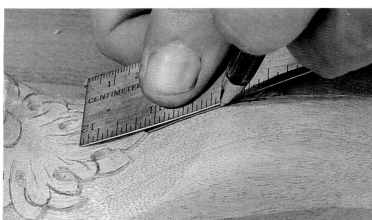

Reestablish the center line in the area where you have carved it away.

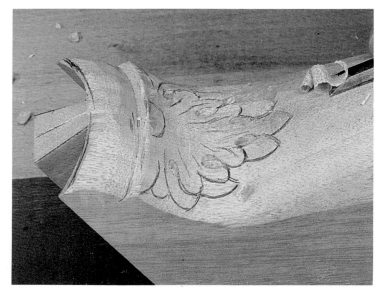

Blend the carved area with the rest of the leg.

Measure down approximately 1 1/4" from bottom of the leaf carving and make a mark on the center line.

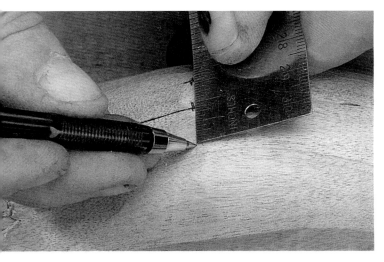

At that point measure 7/16" to either side of the center line and make a mark.

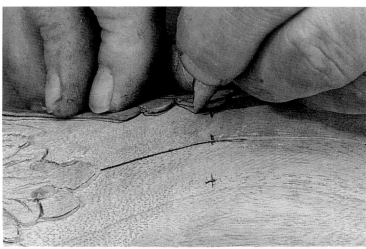

Trace the pattern.

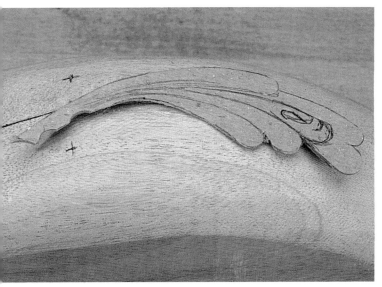

As you can see this pattern is indexed at the top to fit around the previous carving.

Carry it around to the side of the leg.

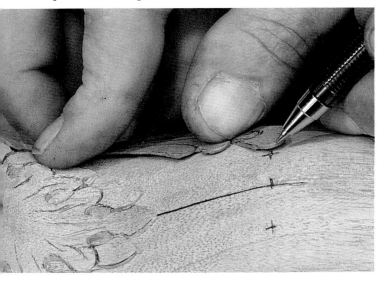

Line up the indexing, and placing the tip of the foliage so it meets the mark you made.

This pattern has an overlapping leaf. Drive a chisel here...

and at the end of the leaf.

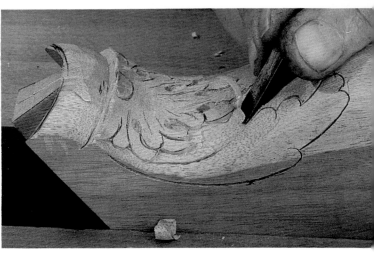

Carve the field beside the leaves.

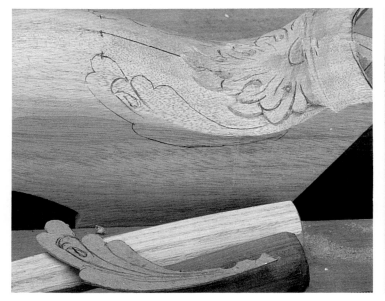

Refer to the pattern and draw in the details.

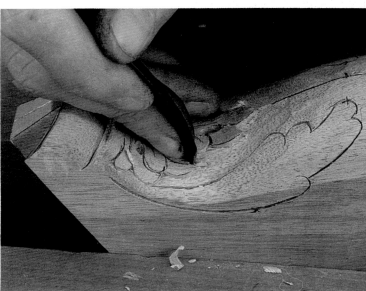

In the area between the groups of leaves you may need to set the first carving deeper. Do this by hand, pressing in as you need to.

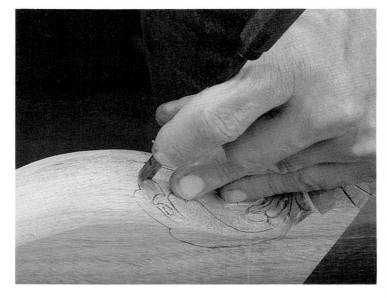

Set the pattern in the same way you did on the earlier foliage, using matching gouges.

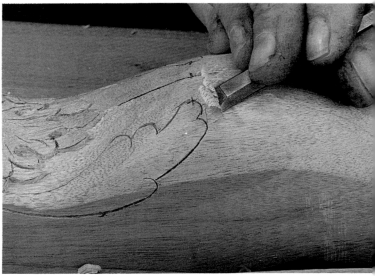

Continue to work your way around.

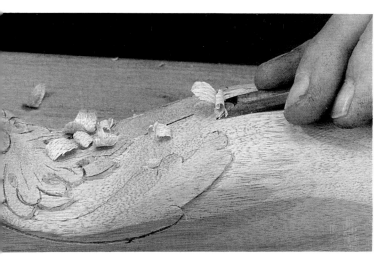

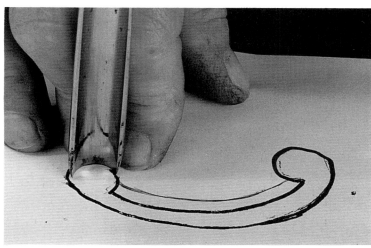

Trim across to the other side. You do this to be sure you have a nice shape to the knee. Unfortunately this means you will need to reestablish your center line. Repeat the relief process on the other side.

Cut out the c-scroll pattern using gouges that match its sweeps.

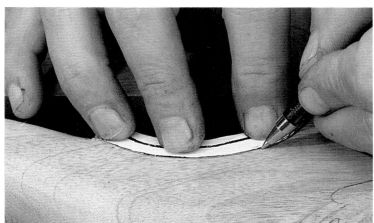

Align the pattern and draw the outside line. Flip the pattern over and repeat on the other side.

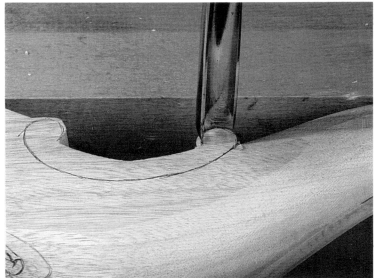

Progress.

Set the pattern using the matching chisels.

I trim back to the scroll using a flat chisel and taking a light cut starting at the dovetail edge.

At the lower point of upper foliage make a mark 3/8" from each side of the center line.

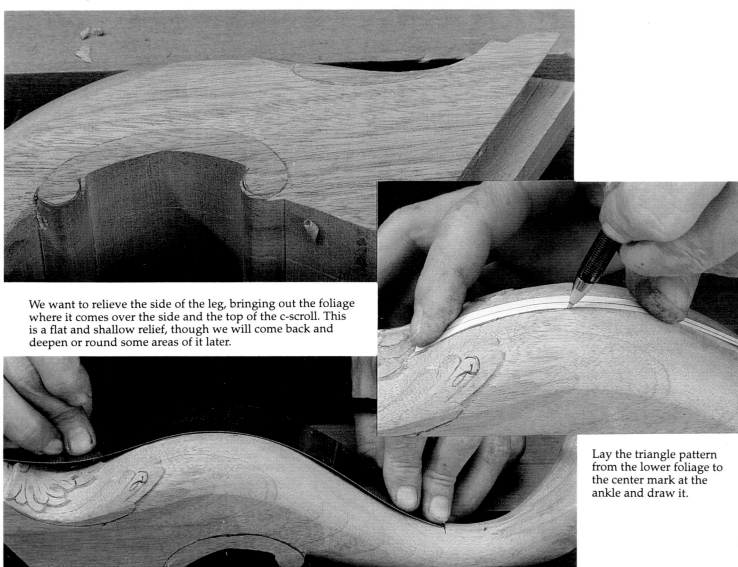

We want to relieve the side of the leg, bringing out the foliage where it comes over the side and the top of the c-scroll. This is a flat and shallow relief, though we will come back and deepen or round some areas of it later.

Lay the triangle pattern from the lower foliage to the center mark at the ankle and draw it.

Following the contour of the leg, measure along the center line to a point 8" below the tip of upper foliage. Mark the ankle.

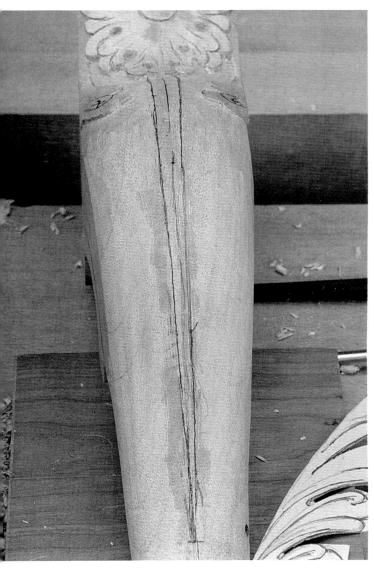

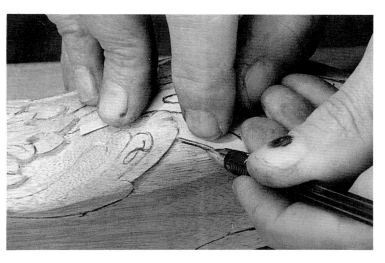

Draw the pattern on the knee. Drawing the pattern directly, takes about a million fingers. Since you only have ten or so, make sure the pattern stays aligned with the side of the long triangle as you draw.

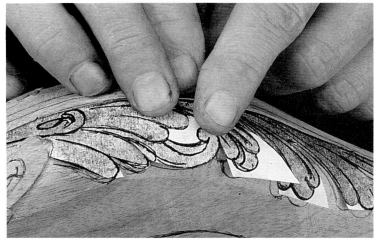

The triangle.

The other option is to stick the pattern to the work with rubber cement.

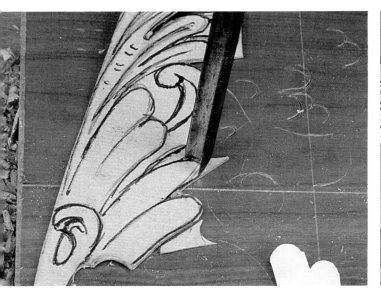

Copy the lower foliage pattern, cut around it, and trim it with matching gouges, as you did with the previous patterns.

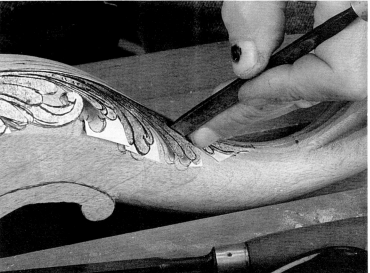

With the pattern glued in place you can set it in lightly with the appropriate gouges.

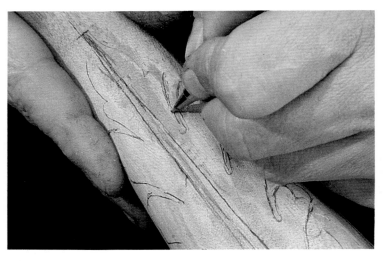

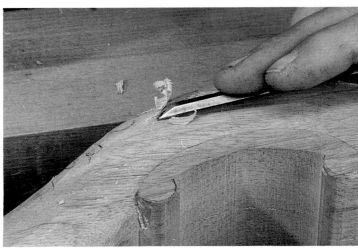

When the lines are established, remove the pattern and go over the lines with pencil for easier reference. Then set the outlines with a chisel to create a stop.

Carve around the foliage to relieve it.

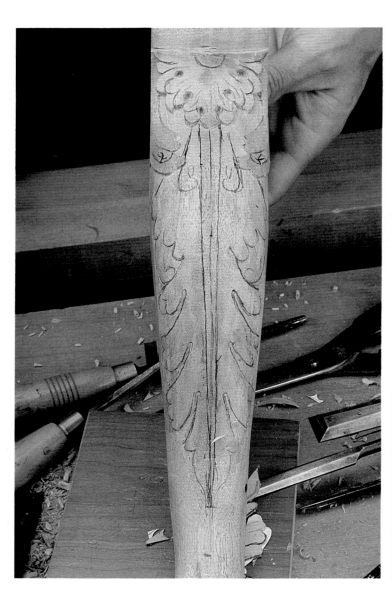

Ready to remove the ground.

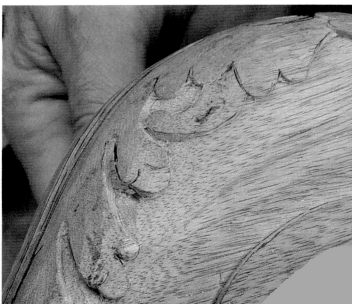

The foliage emerges.

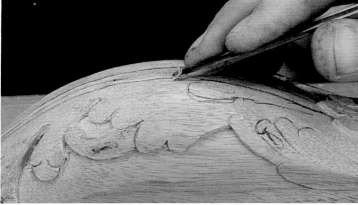

With a No. 2/11 veiner, outline the long V.

The V defined.

As with the other foliage, you will see from the pattern that some fronds are above others. Begin carving with those that are above the rest, like this one. Use a gouge to define the shape with a stop...

and cut back to it from the lower leaves.

Again, as you come back to the side foliage that you carved before, you may need to deepen your earlier lines to allow for this new dimension.

Round over this upper frond using a gouge with the cup against the work.

Refer to the pattern and draw the lines of the rest of the foliage.

Begin the modeling at the triangular spaces between the leaf fronds. On the concave edge of the upper leaf drive the appropriately sized gouge nearly straight into the line.

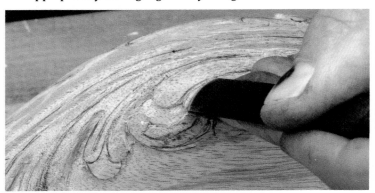

On the facing, convex edge of the lower frond place the gouge with the cup against the edge, angle it down and drive back to the first cut.

Two things happen. The triangle pops out, and the lower frond, because it was cut at an angle, seems to go under the upper, giving you a feel of dimensionality.

Shape the fronds by going down their center with a gouge.

This series of four leaves is done.

Some of the fronds are in profile, giving them an almost hooded effect. The inside of these is carved out with a thin veiner...

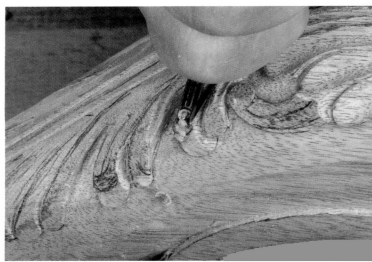

This is also a useful tool for cupping out some of the narrower fronds.

The hooded portion of the profiled fronds is achieved with the gouge, holding the cup against the work as you carve.

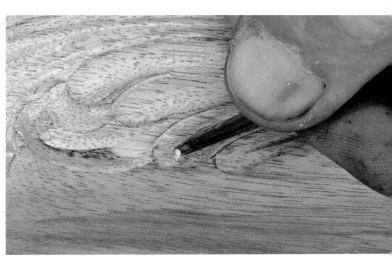

Add veins down the center of the fronds.

Continue until all the fronds are shaped.

Model the top and side foliage in the same way.

One side complete, repeat all the steps on the other.

Set stops at the circular ends of the c-scroll.

The result.

With the appropriate gouge run along the lower edge of the C, starting at one end, going half way...

Run a small incised line above this trough with a veiner. This helps to define the curve. Again come from both ends to the middle.

and coming back from the other end.

Round over the C using a gouge with the cup against the surface. Start at the middle and work to the outside to avoid grain problems.

Round over the ends.

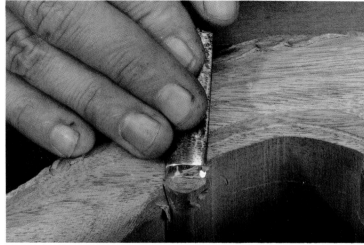

Blend the surface back to the C scroll.

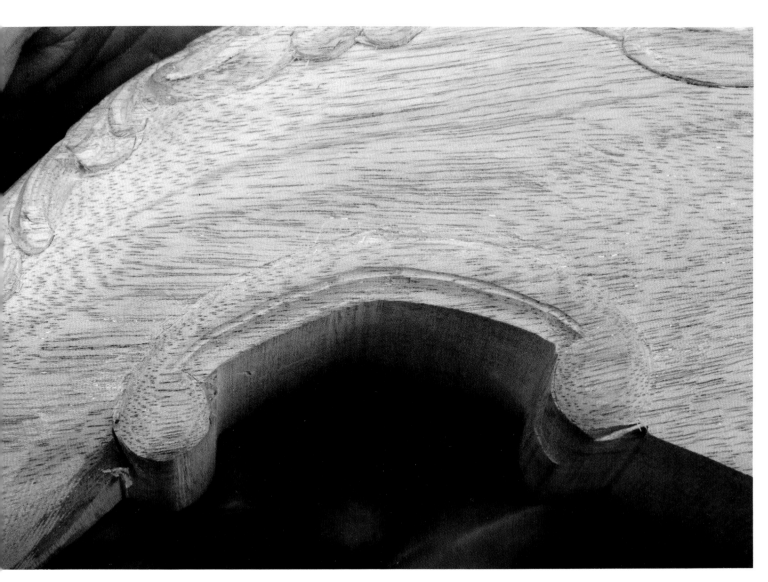

The C scroll finished.

The table top is made from two pieces of straight grained mahogany, joined together to create a piece 31 3/4" wide. Typically these table tops were between 30" and 35" wide. If your piece is different than the one we are using, you will need to make adjustments to the pattern for the edge.

The glue joint provides one center line between the two boards. Draw the other center across the grain, using a square.

Use the combination square and a straight edge to divide the for corner segments in half diagonally from the center.

Divide the arcs in half to get your marks to get 16 segments in the circle.

Draw the circumference of the top. This is the low tech way to do it. This circle is 31 3/4" in diameter.

Connect the marks through the center to bisect the segments.

The result is a circle with 16 equal segments.

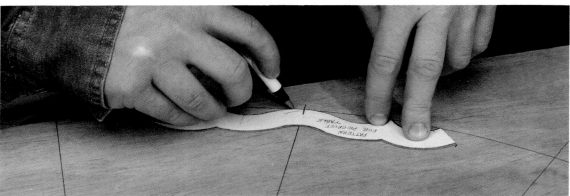

The scalloped pattern is drawn with its center on alternating rays around the table top.

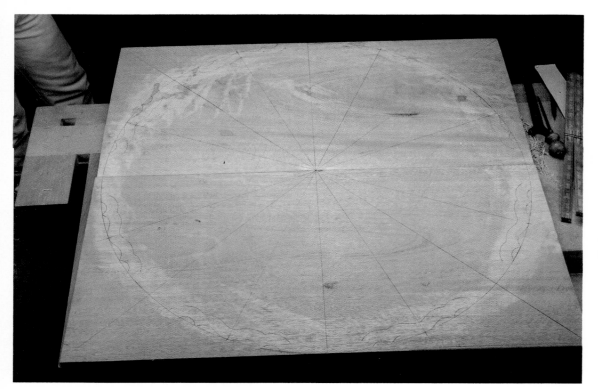

Complete layout of the scalloped pattern.

Set the compass to the end of the inside of the scallop pattern and use it to connect with the next scallop, forming the inside rim of the top.

The center of the table will be routed out to the inside point of the pattern. You can draw a circle if you want, but the jig we use for the router should establish the limits without it. Measure from the center to this point. In this case it is about 14 3/4".

Route a circle about 1/32" less than the 3/8" final depth. This allows for clean-up and scraping. Make sure the top is clamped securely, and make sure the bit and everything else is tightened. A test run for safety and to check equipment is suggested.

To take away the center we use a plunge router with a 1 1/4" straight bit with a 1/2" shank. A smaller bit can be used, but will take much longer. We made a trammel arm for the router from fiberboard. This is attached to the shoe of the router. Measure from the far edge of the cutting blade back 14 1/2" and drill a hole. This will be the center of the of the table top, and using this as a pivot we will create a circle that will be slightly smaller in diameter than the inner edge of the scallop pattern. This gives you a little leeway for mistakes.

Put a screw through the trammel into the center of your table top. It should go in no more than 3/8", which will be our router depth.

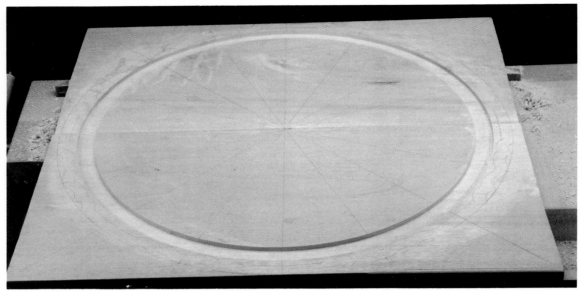

The result is a 1 1/4" groove to define the inside edge of the scalloped pattern.

Cut around table top, leaving the line. We use a jig saw for this step, and begin by cutting the original plain circle first. This relieves the wood and allows us to cut the pattern more easily.

Cut the curves of the scallop, leaving them full.

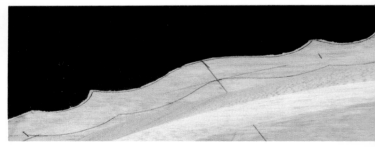

Continue at each scallop.

Cut relief cuts into the valleys of the scallop patterns.

Use a pattern maker's rasp to true up the edge, cleaning to the line.

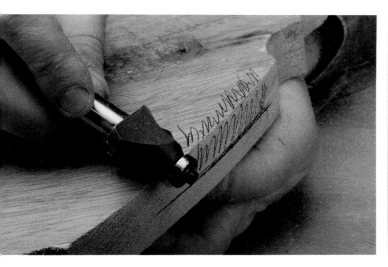

Turn the top over. We want to chamfer the bottom edge to about 1/2" inch from the top, which we will need for future router work. The bit is a 1", 45 degree piloted chamfering bit, with a ball bearing guide.

Work your way around the bottom edge...

for this result.

This will be chamfered further by hand. The router just takes away some of the tedium.

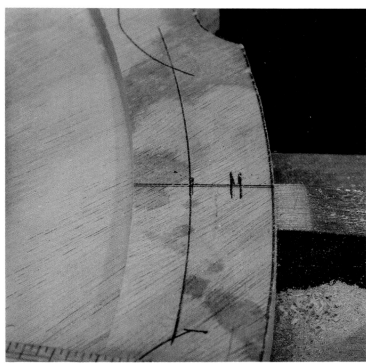

Turn the top right side up. We are going to bead the edge. But first we need to mark the width of the bead. Here you see how we figured it. Working out from the inside of the rim, the first shape is a cove, which is 1/2 the thickness of the rim. Next is a thin fillet, 1/16". The remaining rim is a bead, which in this case is 15/16" wide.

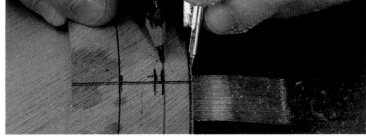

Set a scribe for the width of the bead and draw it all around the top.

With a 3/16" piloted round-over bit, go around the top edge of the table top. The blade should be set so that this corner is flush with the surface of the wood.

Work your way around the table top. You can see why we left the center of the table top intact. It provides the surface for the router bed.

Mark the width of the fillet at an innermost point of the scalloped pattern.

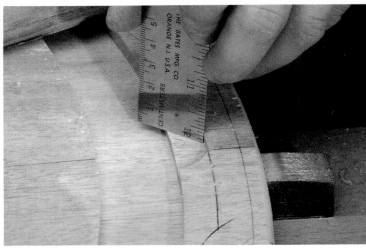

Using the 1 1/4" cutter, set the trammel so the router will cut a circle to the innermost diameter of the fillet ring. In this case, measuring a little inside the diameter of the fillet for safety, it measures 15 1/8". The depth of the cut is just shy of 3/16". Starting in a straight section and measuring will allow you to check your settings. Since this part will be removed in the end, you can spot mistakes before they matter.

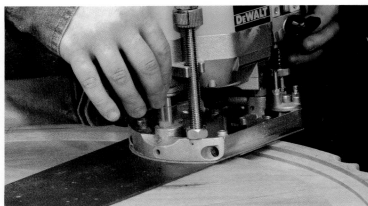

When things are correct, continue to cut around the rim.

Switch to a 3/8" straight bit to follow the line of the bead. This is done at the same depth as the previous cut, just shy of 3/16", and is a freehand cut. Come right to the inside line of the bead.

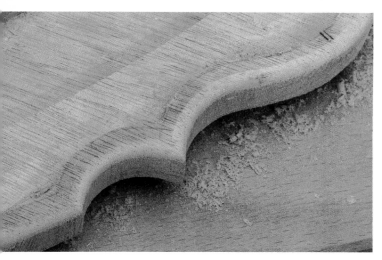

The result. The rest will be done by hand.

The result.

While the center of the top is still intact, turn it over to finish the chamfering of the edge. The center will support the work while you work. Begin by scribing a line about 1" from the edge, all around. This line will mark the point where the chamfer begins.

When the rough shape is established, refine it with a pattern maker's rasp. You then move to finer and finer wood files to smooth it.

Round the bottom edge over. I begin with a chisel, which removes a lot of wood fairly easily.

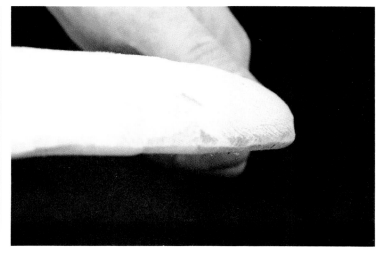

A view from the side.

Redraw the inside of the scallop pattern.

The result.

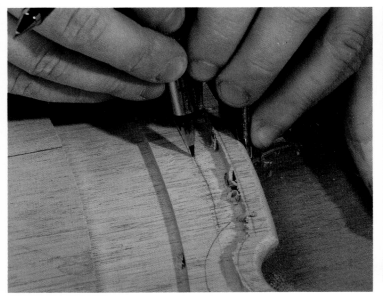

Connect the inside line between the scallops using a scribe set to the correct distance and running along the edge.

With the router it is now time to remove the waste from the center of the table top. Go across the grain using the 1 1/4" straight bit.

Cut freehand with the router to the inside line of the rim, going to the level you earlier established for the center portion of the table.

You must leave these bridges every few inches to support the router.

One side done. Repeat on the other.

Use a chisel, beveled side against the table top, to remove the bridges. The rough cut you can drive with a mallet.

One side completely done.

The finishing cut can be done by pushing the chisel through the wood.

To true up the rim we use gouges with matching sweeps, and a selection of chisels.

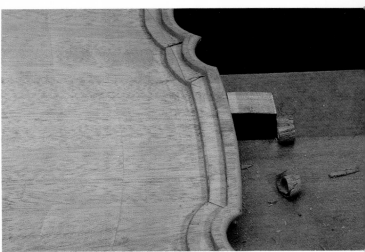

Progress. I've drawn in the lines that set apart the various sections of the rim.

Truing the rim is simply a matter of selecting a gouge that matches a particular curve and pushing it along the edge to create the shape. Be sure not to undercut the rim. Keep the handle vertical or leaning slightly toward the outside.

The molding is shaped with a 8/13mm gouge, and with 25/6mm and 28/6mm back bent gouges.

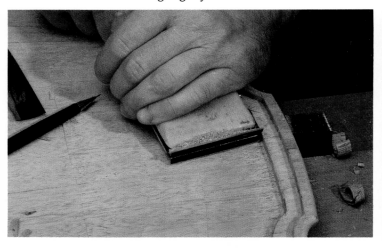

Clean up the surface with a scraper. Before using these commercial scrapers I file them, use a stone on them, and polish them up.

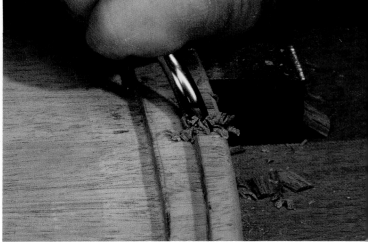

The back bent gouge is used to round the inside edge of the outer bead.

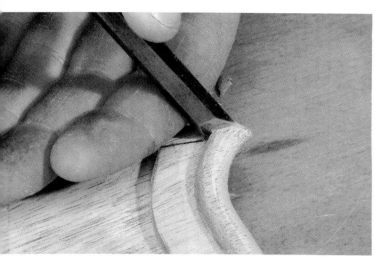

At the corner use a straight chisel to sever the grain of the wood. Don't go too deeply, but gently rock your chisel along the line.

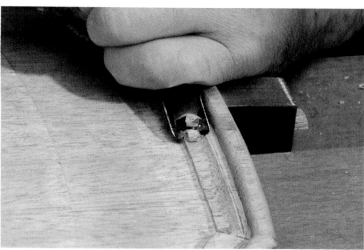

Use the #8 gouge carve the cove. Leave a small (less than 1/16) edge above the surface of the table top to create a shadow line. This gives a nice deep curve.

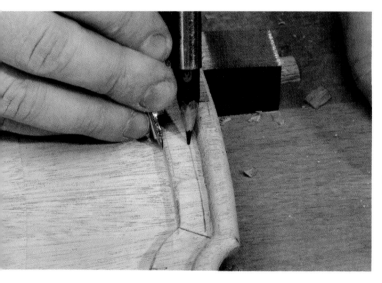

Use a scribe to set the width of the fillet at a little less than 1/16" from the outer bead.

Flatten the cove with a #7 gouge.

Set the corners of the cove in the same way as the bead.

Smooth the surface of the table top with a scraper that has been sharpened to remove a nice curl rather than dust. This can either be a pull-type scraper with a handle...

or a traditional cabinet scraper.

After scraping, sand the whole table top with progressively finer paper. I begin with 100 grit on a random orbital sander, followed by 150, without over sanding. We want to keep some of the irregularities that come with hand construction.

The bead, fillet, cove, and table surface defined.

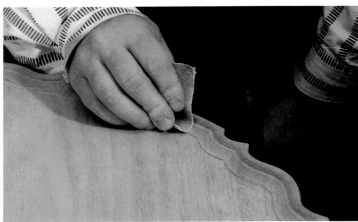

Sand the molded rim and the tight corners by hand. Remember to sand the bottom side of the top.

Ready for finishing.

These are the plates for the bird cage. They are essentially eight inches square, except that bottom piece has ears at one edge that are 10 inches wide and come up the side 7/8". The ears will be rounded and need to have the grain running through them.

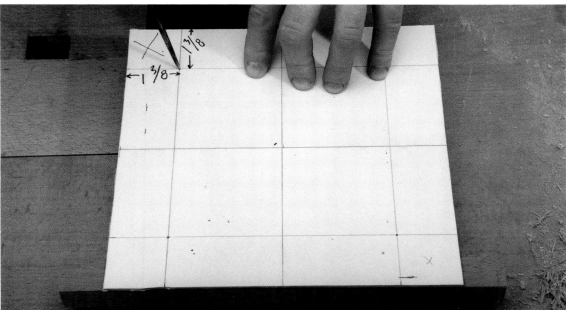

An 8" x 8" template is useful, with lines 1 3/8" in from each edge crossing to tell you where the spindles will be place, and a mark in the middle. An x in one corner will assure that your orientation stays the same with the two boards.

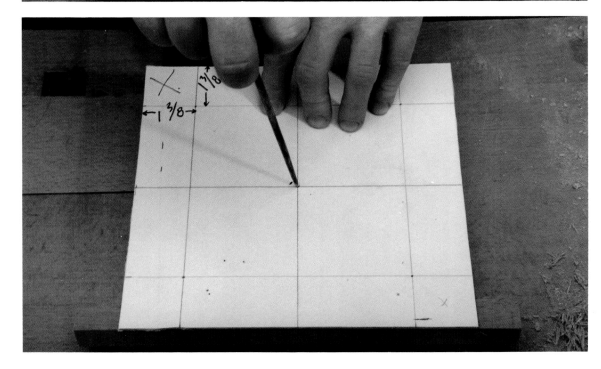

Use an awl to mark the center and the spindle positions on the **top** sides of the upper and lower plates.

The center hole in the upper plate does not go all the way through, so we need to turn it over, lay the template so it stays in the same orientation and mark the center. The center hole in the underside of the upper plate is 1" in diameter and goes in 3/8".

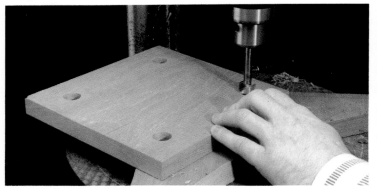

Drill 5/8" holes completely through the upper and lower plates for the spindle tenons.

Drill a 1" hole in the center of bottom side of the upper plate, going 3/8" deep.

Make a 1 1/2" hole all the way through the lower plate.

Find the center of the trunnions...

and scribe the trunnion so the diameter matches the thickness of the birdcage plates, approximately 7/8".

116

Begin by rounding the edge of the **upper** side of the plate to match the circumference.

Make a stop cut.

Use a chisel to round the inside corners of the trunnions. Be sure to put a stop at the bottom of this cut before doing it.

and round the corner back to it.

For the last corner carry the line of the side of the plate around using a square.

Test the size of the trunnion by fitting it in a 7/8" hole drilled in scrap. Adjust as necessary. You notice that I have drilled the hole so it opens up across the end of the board. The reason for this will be clear later.

Set the strike plate for the catch in the top side of the upper plate of the birdcage. Center the plate on the edge...

and come back to it from the top.

Mark the position on the edge of the plate with an knife.

Now go right to the line and clean up the mortise, establishing a depth the matches the thickness of the hardware.

We want to set the face side first. This is cut with the same procedures you would use for a hinge. Cut the outline...

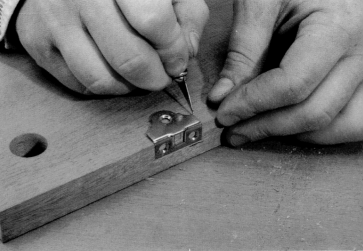

With the square part of the strike plate in place, trace around the decorative curved part.

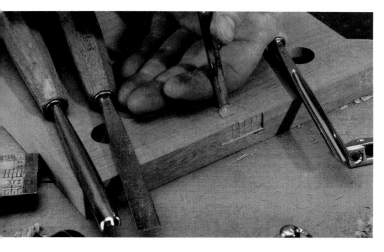

Set the lines with matching gouges, pushing straight in.

Mark the opening in the strike plate...

Clean it up with chisels, again matching the depth to the thickness of the hardware.

saw on the lines...

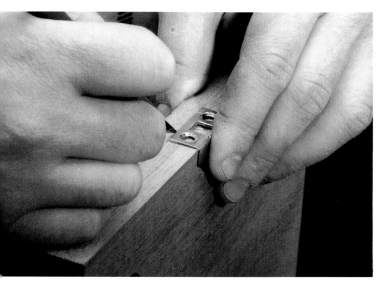

Now, with the curved section in place, you can reset the line on the other side to its final dimension and clean it out.

and chip it out.

Round all four edges of the lower plate. On the end grain be careful not ot go all the way through or you will have tear out. Go part way, turn the piece, and go the other way.

Assemble the bird cage.

Cut the spindles apart.

Apply glue to the wedges...

and drive them home.

Cut a slot for the wedge in each end of the spindles. These should stop about 1/8" above the first element of the turning and **must** go across the grain. The cuts at each end should be on the same line.

Trim the end of the spindles...

and smooth them with a chisel. Then you can prepare the surfaces of the birdcage for finishing.

Before cutting the washer from the turning stock, cut a 1 1/2" hole through its center.

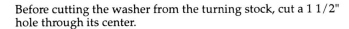

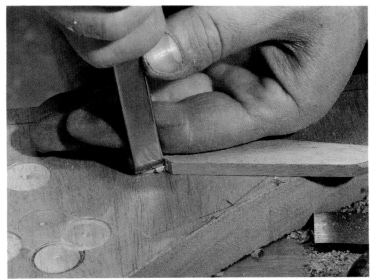

Saw the washer from the stock. Sand the surfaces of the washer.

Cut the key on the bandsaw from a piece of 1/4" mahogany and clean it up with a chisel and sandpaper.

Align the key across the grain of the washer so that it is centered.

Mark the sides of the key on the washer.

and with a 1/4" chisel clean out the slot.

Cut slightly inside the lines down to the bottom of the fillet.

Put the washer in place, aligning the slot with one of the legs of the table. Mark the position of the slot on the post. This will be the lower edge of a through mortise which will hold the key.

True the lines with a chisel...

Draw a center line on the post, oriented with the center of the leg.

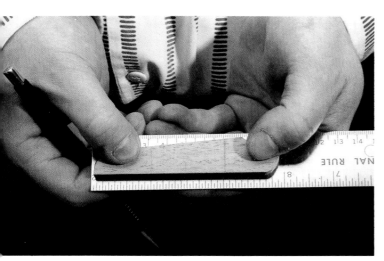

Mark the center of the key, and draw perpendicular lines from the straight edge to the top, 3/4" from the center on each side. These are the lines where the key will enter and emerge from the post.

With a 1/4" bit, drill through the post. Begin at the level, bottom line...

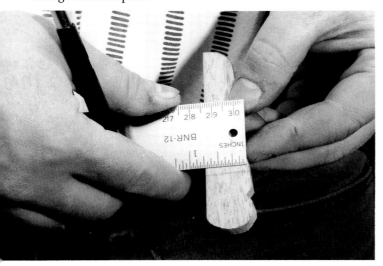

Measure the lines...

and work your way up to the slanted top line.

and transfer one to one side of the post and the other to the other side. This will define the shape of your through mortise. The wide end of the mortise will be 3/4"" in this case, and the narrow, emerging end of the mortise is 5/8".

Clean up the mortise with a chisel.

Check for fit and make adjustments.

Draw around the cage, and mark the center of the trunnion.

The bird cage assembled.

Draw a line between the trunnion centers.

Center the birdcage on the bottom of the table top.

Arrange the battens so the crowning is the opposite of the table top's. This way, if there is any warping, the two will fight against each other, keeping things straight. Mark the trunnion center on the batten.

The result.

Draw a line up from the trunnion center and measure 7/16" from the edge. This is the center of the hole for the trunnion.

Position the birdcage and battens, then mark the length of the battens at the place where they meet the bevel of the table top. Mark both sides, the outside edge will be shorter than the inside.

Clamp the two battens together so the holes align. Use a 7/8" Forstner bit to drill the two holes. These will break out of the edges of the batten, which is what you want.

Lay the patterns on the inside surface, giving you the longest dimension. Cut the batten ends on the bandsaw.

Chamfer the top edges of the battens using a router or plane.

Screw in place with no glue. Be sure the screws are the correct length, so they don't come through the top of the table.

Lay the batten in place and mark where the outside edge of the end needs to be rounded off. Shape it with chisel or rasp.

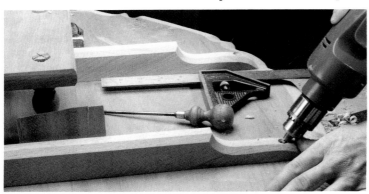

The batten is attached to the table top with three screws, one in the center, and one about 1 1/4" from the end. The end screws are angled slightly in. Put a piece of veneer or 1/16" poster board between the batten and the birdcage as a spacer, and drill pilot holes.

The batten and birdcage assembly in place.

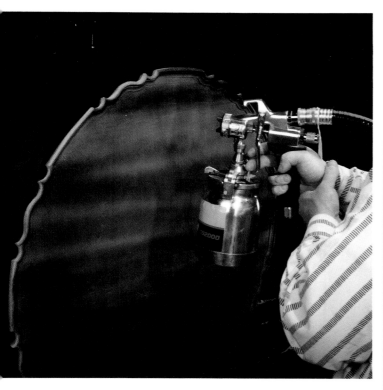

We are using a spray stain for the table top. It gives a nice even finish which we prefer. If you don't have the spray equipment, it is fine to use the traditional brush method. Which ever you choose, it is best to test the stain first on a piece of scrap. We spray two coats, letting things dry in between.

Several thin coats of shellac follow...

This is rubbed down with a fine pad of Scotchbrite™.

with a rubdown between each coat.

Continue until you have a nice rich finish.

A final rubdown with 0000 steel wool...

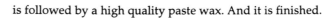

is followed by a high quality paste wax. And it is finished.

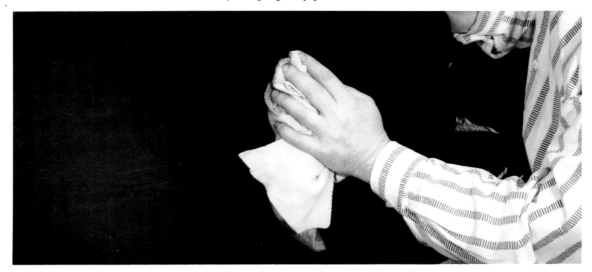

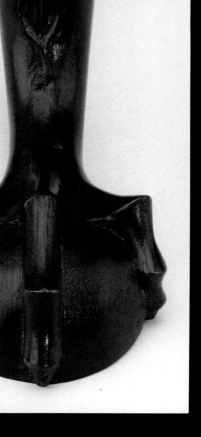

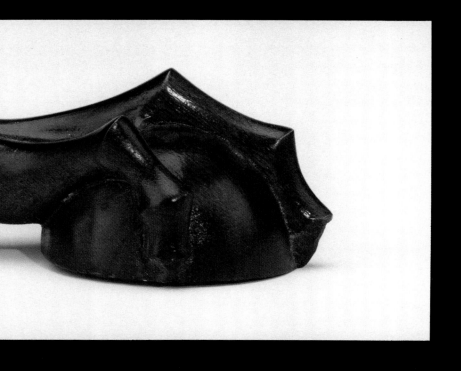

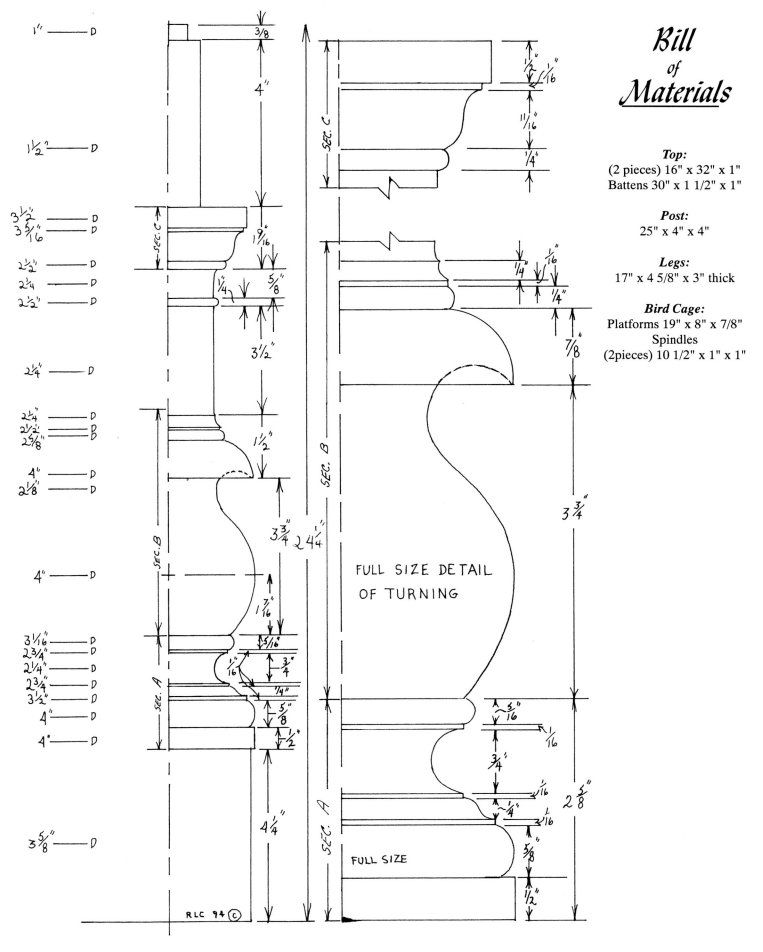

Bill
of
Materials

Top:
(2 pieces) 16" x 32" x 1"
Battens 30" x 1 1/2" x 1"

Post:
25" x 4" x 4"

Legs:
17" x 4 5/8" x 3" thick

Bird Cage:
Platforms 19" x 8" x 7/8"
Spindles
(2pieces) 10 1/2" x 1" x 1"

FULL SIZE DETAIL
OF TURNING

FULL SIZE

RLC 94 ©

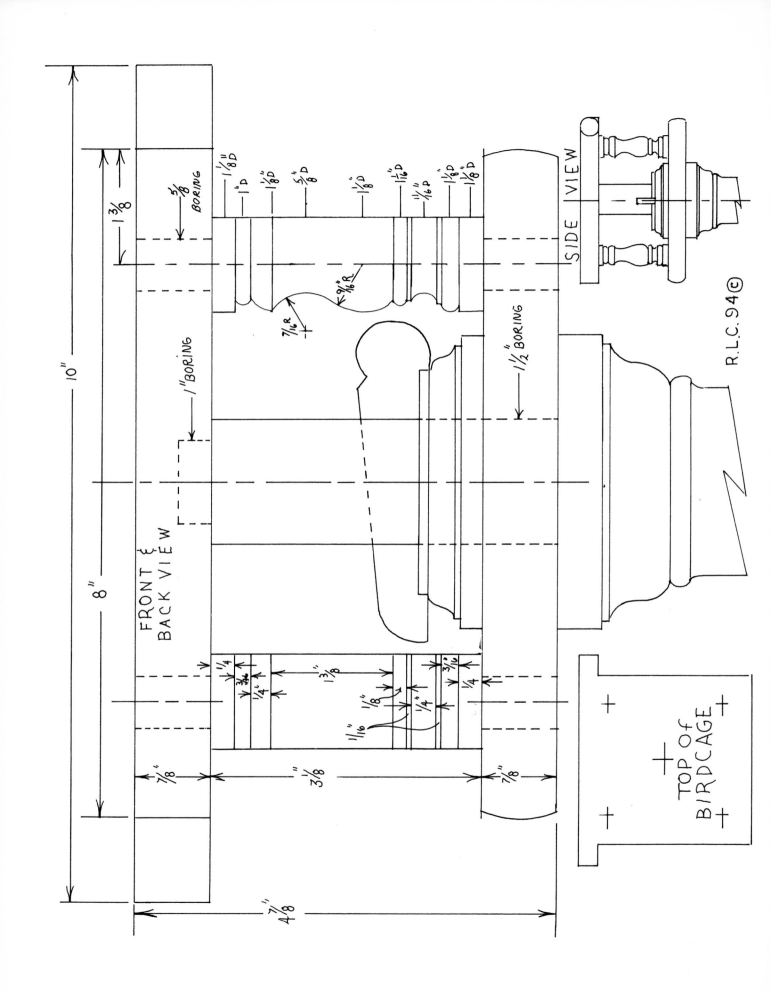

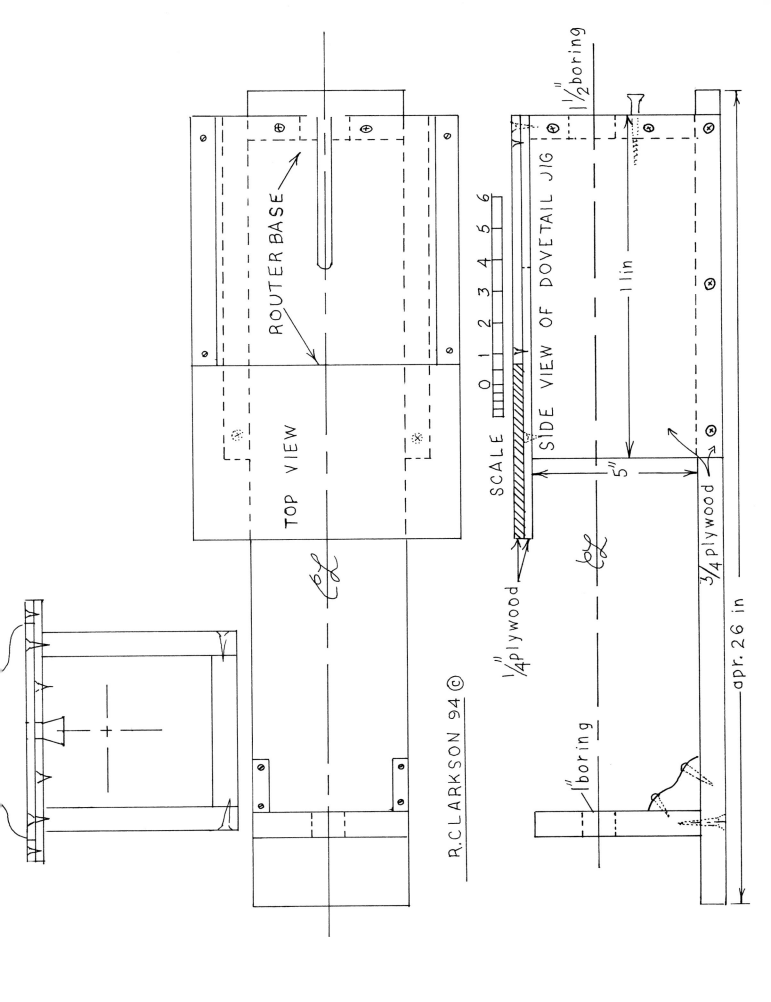

ROUTER BASE

TOP VIEW

SCALE 0 1 2 3 4 5 6

SIDE VIEW OF DOVETAIL JIG

R.CLARKSON 94 ©

1½" boring

¼" plywood

11 in

5"

¾" plywood

1" boring

apr. 26 in

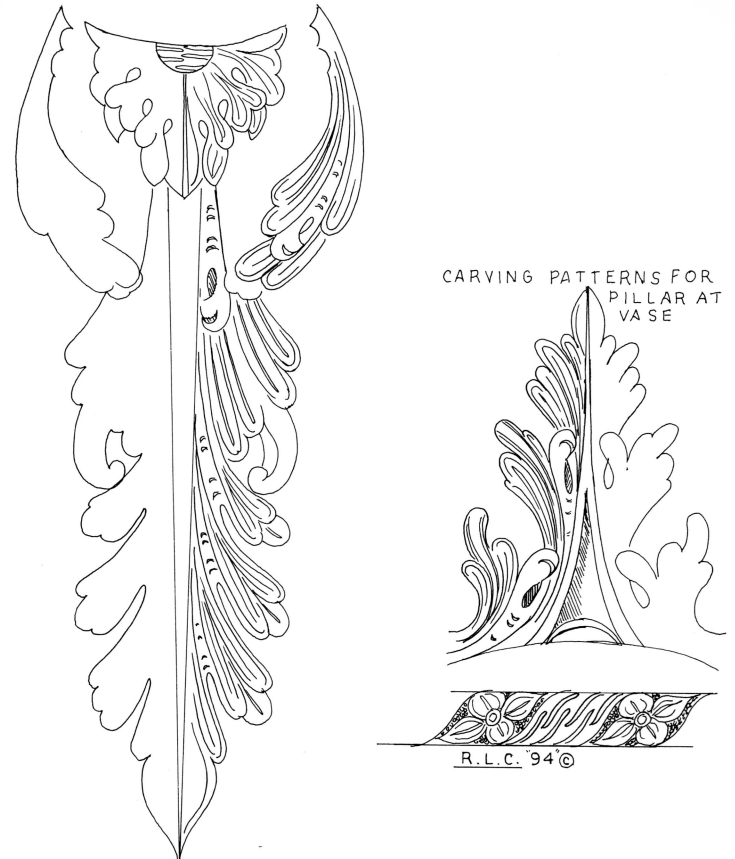

CARVING PATTERNS FOR
PILLAR AT
VASE

R.L.C. "94" ©

CARVING PATTERNS FOR
LEG. COPY, CUT OUT, AND
PASTE ON LEG WITH
RUBBER CEMENT

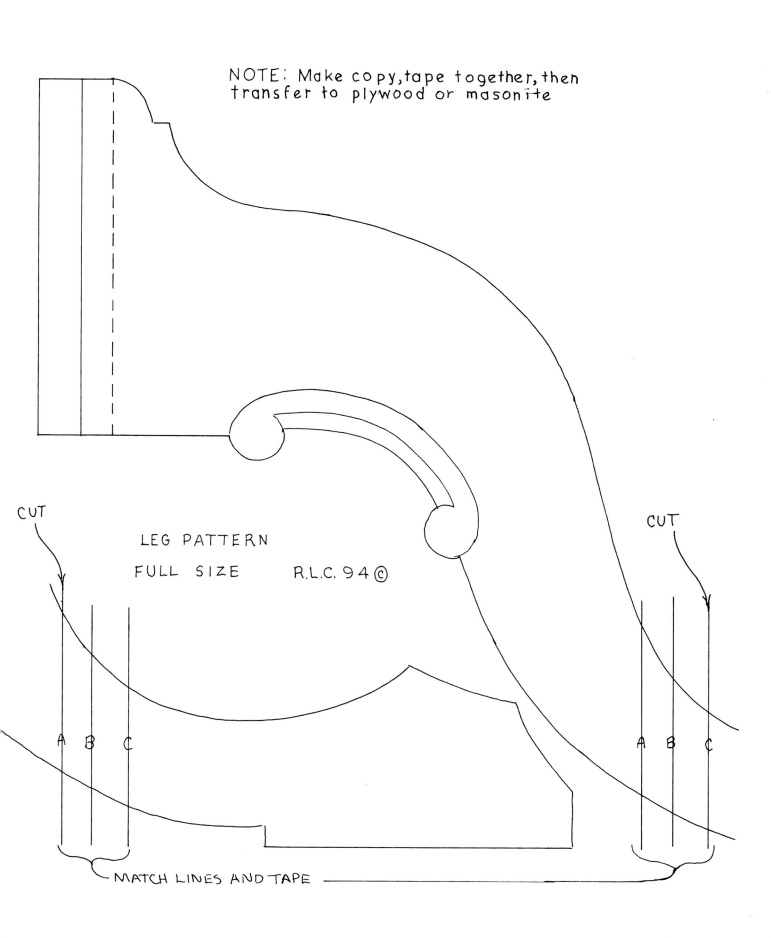

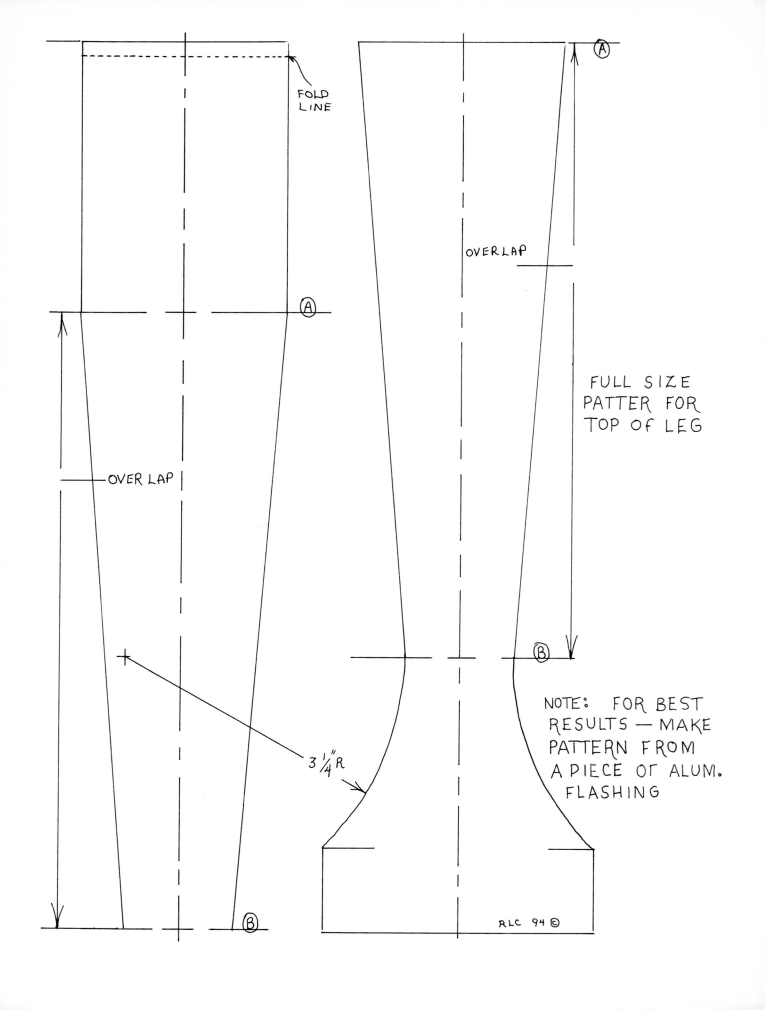

FOLD LINE

Ⓐ

OVER LAP

3¼"R

Ⓑ

OVERLAP

Ⓐ

FULL SIZE PATTER FOR TOP OF LEG

Ⓑ

NOTE: FOR BEST RESULTS — MAKE PATTERN FROM A PIECE OF ALUM. FLASHING

RLC 94 ©

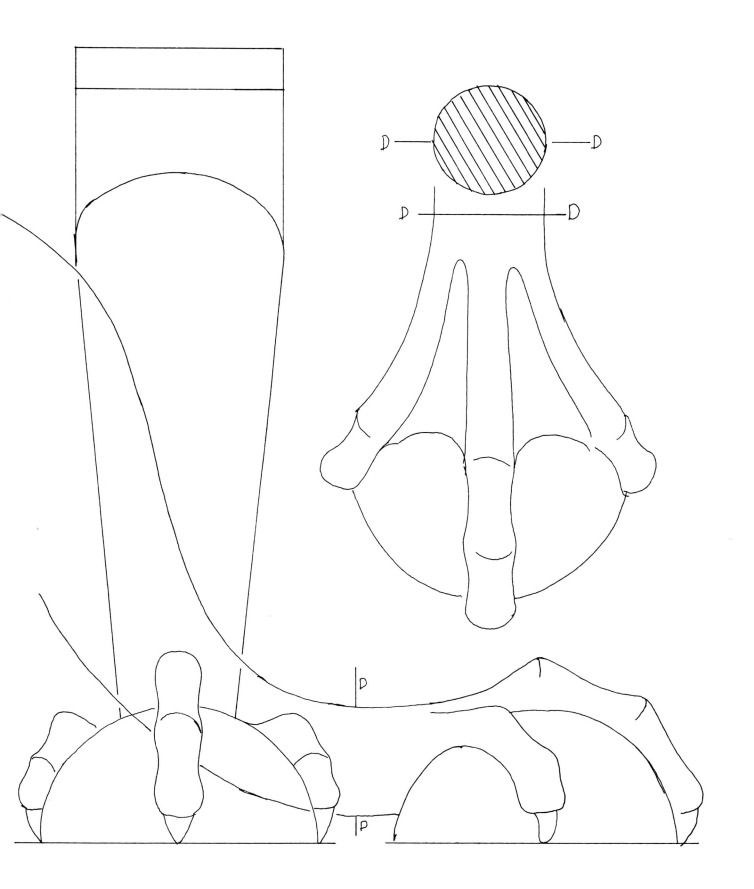

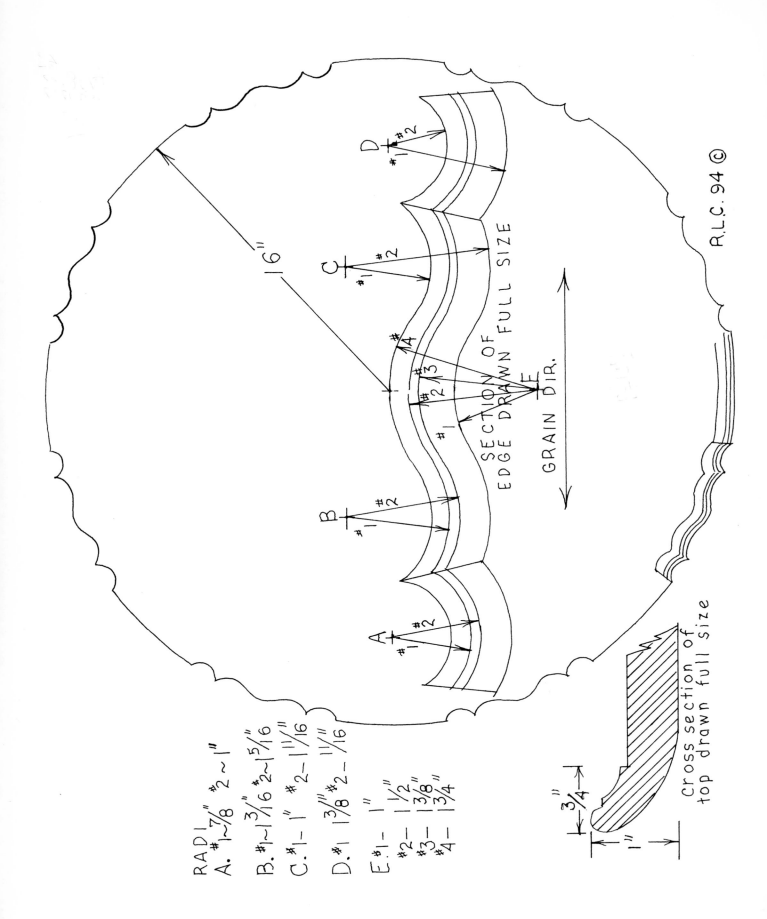

RADI

A. #1 ~ 7/8" #2 ~ 1"

B. #1 ~ 3/16" #2 ~ 1 5/16"

C. #1 - 1" #2 - 1 11/16"

D. #1 - 1 3/8" #2 - 11/16"

E. #1 - 1 1/2"
   #2 - 1 3/8"
   #3 - 1 3/8"
   #4 - 3/4"

16"

SECTION OF EDGE DRAWN FULL SIZE

GRAIN DIR.

Cross section of top drawn full size

3/4"

1"

R.L.C. 94 ©

144